THE
TACTICAL
RIFLE

For Evie and Eric—
may their elephants always be in the zoo . . .

. . . and to Cheryl
for always listening and understanding.

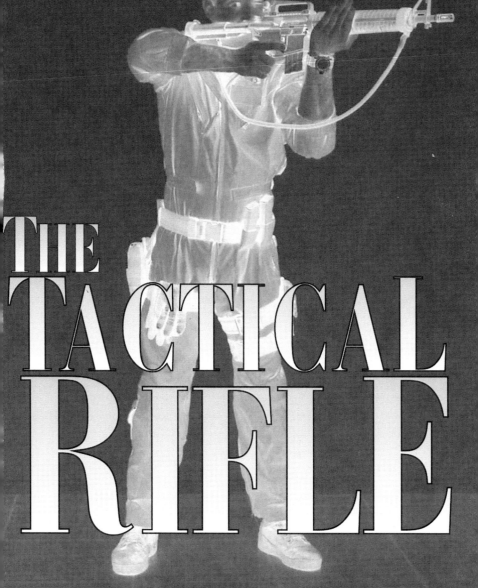

GABRIEL SUAREZ

The Precision Tool for Urban Police Operations

THE TACTICAL RIFLE

Also by Gabriel Suarez:
Close-Range Gunfighting (video)
The Combative Perspective
Force-on-Force Gunfight Training
Tactical Advantage
Tactical Pistol (also available in Spanish edition, La Pistola Táctica)
Tactical Pistol Marksmanship
Tactical Shotgun

The Tactical Rifle: The Precision Tool for Urban Police Operations
by Gabriel Suarez

Copyright © 1999 by Gabriel Suarez
ISBN 13: 978-1-58160-049-0
Printed in the United States of America

Published by Paladin Press, a division of
Paladin Enterprises, Inc.,
Gunbarrel Tech Center
7077 Winchester Circle
Boulder, Colorado 80301 USA
+1.303.443.7250

Direct inquiries and/or orders to the above address.

PALADIN, PALADIN PRESS, and the "horse head" design
are trademarks belonging to Paladin Enterprises and
registered in United States Patent and Trademark Office.

Visit our website at www.paladin-press.com.

Table of Contents

Warning

Firearms are potentially dangerous and must be handled responsibly by individual trainees and experienced shooters alike. The technical information presented here on firearms handling, training, and shooting inevitably reflects the authors' beliefs and experience with particular firearms and training techniques under specific circumstances that the reader cannot duplicate exactly. Therefore, the information in this book is presented *for academic study only* and should be approached with great caution. This book is not intended to serve as a replacement for professional instruction under a qualified instructor.

Acknowledgments

Primarily, and above all, I must thank Lt. Mike Beautz, commanding officer of our agency's Tactical Rifle Team, for his support and for his uncommon faith in his men. It was he who took on the near-Herculean task of convincing the department that we must have rifles, and that I must be the one to teach and develop the team. Mike is the quintessential been-there-done-that warrior-leader in a profession that is increasingly lacking in men of his caliber!

Additional thanks must go to my rifle partners, Officer Alfred Acosta, Officer Rick Crocker, Officer Carl Heublein, and Range Master Jason Mann, and, of course, to our "Procurement Officer," Greg McElveen. These men provided great assistance to the Rifle Team Project, as well

x | **The Tactical Rifle**

as to the research culminating in this volume. Mention must
also be made of my partners on the Sierra Team, primarily Sgt.
Hank Ramirez and Officer Mike Graham, as well as the volunteers of the SMPD Tactical Rifle Team Alpha and Bravo
Groups, and to Cory Trapp of SAS Products and Harry Lu of
Stembridge Arms for their supply of unusual weapons.

Finally, I must thank the late Officer Mitch Kato of the
SMPD for his help with many of the photographs. Kato-San
had to leave early, and we will miss him.

"We few, we happy few, we band of brothers . . ."
                                        — *King Henry V*, Act 4, Scene 3

Preface

My good friend Jeff Cooper once called the rifle "The Queen of Weapons" because of its versatility. In the pantheon of weapons, the rifle truly does more things well than any other weapon. But within that versatility, there is also, inevitably, a degree of specialization.

When the focus of that specialization is personal combat, the number of suitable rifles grows smaller. Note that any rifle can be pressed into such service in a pinch, but some rifles are specifically designed for the combative mission. Even within the scope of that mission, however, choosing a weapon demands a clear understanding of the operator's needs. The mission of a military sniper, for example, is drastically different from that of a lone rural patrol deputy, just as the role of

February 1997 – North Hollywood, California.

Urban police agency is introduced to rifle combat.

The answer is in the state-of-the-art equipment and modern training, as seen in this session of the SMPD Patrol Rifle Team Training School. (Photo courtesy of Officer Mitch Kato.)

The author, Officer Gabe Suarez, was tasked with researching the mission and developing a doctrine for the rifle in urban law enforcement.

a containment officer attached to a SWAT unit is different from that of those who "go inside." In this book we are concerned with the role and mission of the tactical rifle, particularly pertaining to urban police operations. Although many rural departments have deployed rifles for years, this is still a relatively new concept for most large urban agencies.

I remember watching the news footage of the events of 28 February 1997. Two ill-trained and undisciplined aspiring bank robbers were shooting it out with the Los Angeles Police Department (LAPD) officers assigned to the North Hollywood station. I remember thinking, as the courageous members of LAPD SWAT assaulted Larry Phillips' and Emil Matasereano's positions, that urban policing was changing yet again. We'd reached another pivotal moment, and the rifle would inevitably become an ever-present addition to our armories.

Some months later, I was tasked by my agency with developing and instituting a tactical rifle program for patrol first responders. This began an odyssey of research into the "how," "why," and "when" of urban rifle deployment. I researched after-action reports from various agencies, both police and military, foreign and domestic. I spoke with police and military operators who'd used rifles in built-up urban areas. In short, I examined almost all of the available data and doctrine on urban rifle deployments and selected the best ideas.

Having a SWAT as well as a sniper background, not to mention several . . . "critical incidents" under my belt, I looked at everything with the cynical eye of one who really knows "what happens when bullets start flying." The result was that we abandoned many "traditional" rifle techniques and replaced them with new innovative concepts.

My research exposed many myths. One, for example, was the notion that rifles are *long*-range weapons. Urban deployment usually dictates extreme close quarters rather than the traditional extended engagement. Another myth was that rifle rounds will drastically overpenetrate. This was easily dispelled with a study and replication of the Federal Bureau of

Investigation's (FBI's) penetration tests and comparisons of the .223 caliber, as well as conversations with reps from many of the large ammo makers. There were many other misconceptions that faded in the cold light of analysis.

As you read this, a police officer is deploying a rifle against rifle-armed suspects. My prediction is that as we progress into the 21st century, the rifle will again become an integral part of the police operator's tool bag. However, the tools and their intended mission are still selected and instituted by those who do not understand the needs of the operators — those whose real world experience can generously be described as "limited." The result is that the weapons, the selected operators, and the methods of deployment are often ill-advised and ill-conceived . . . if at all.

I am hopeful that this text will serve as a guide to others, making their jobs easier and safer as they make the criminal's job more difficult and more hazardous.

—Officer Gabriel Suarez
HALO Group, Inc., Tactical Training & Consulting
Founder and Senior Tactical Instructor,
SMPD Tactical Rifle Team,
Alpha and Bravo Groups

AN SAS SOLDIER'S PRAYER

I bring this prayer to You, Lord
For You alone can give
What one cannot demand from oneself.
Give me, Lord, what You have left over,
Give me what no one ever asks You for.
I don't ask You for rest,
Or quiet,
Whether of soul or body;
I don't ask You for wealth,
Nor for success, nor even health perhaps.
That sort of thing You get asked for so much
That You can't have any of it left over,
Give me what no one wants from You.
I want insecurity and strife,
And I want You to give me these once and for all.
So that I can be sure of having them always,
Since I shall not always have the courage
To ask You for them.
Give me, Lord, what you have left over,
Give me what others want nothing to do with.
But give me courage too,
And strength and faith;
For You alone can give
What one cannot demand from oneself.

—Lt. Andre Zirnheld, SAS
Killed in Action 26 July 1941

Introduction: Mission and Purpose

*In war there is never any chance for a **second** mistake.*
—Lamarchus (465–414 B.C.)
from Plutarch, *Apothegms*

The police community is very slow to change on some issues. In fact, it has been said that police agencies are driven by "years of tradition unhampered by progress." This is certainly the case when it comes to tactical deployment or concerns about officer safety. Some (although certainly not all) agencies refuse to accept the realities of the job until one of their officers is killed because of inadequate equipment or outdated practices. Then, as they listen to the pipes and watch the honor guard at yet another police funeral, they must face the sobering truth that they themselves are, in part, responsible. As has always been the case in the past, in reaction to the tragedy, things change and another policy is written in blood. This kind of reactive policy making is also apparent when it comes to decisions regarding firearms. Following are some, but certainly not all, of the incidents spanning more than four decades that have brought about a reexamination of the rifle for urban law enforcement:

- Austin, Texas, August 1966—a man named Charles Whitman kills 15 citizens and wounds 31 others in a 96-minute fusillade from a 28-story tower that was to be remembered as the "Texas Tower Incident."
- New Orleans, Louisiana, August 1974—23-year-old Jimmy Essex kills 7 and wounds another 21 people in a Howard Johnson's motel. Essex sustained fire for 11 hours with a rifle.
- Miami, Florida, April 1986—Rifle-equipped robbers Platt and Matix engage pistol- and shotgun-armed FBI agents in a close-range firefight. FBI agents finally neutralize the suspects, but not without incurring heavy losses.
- North Hollywood, California, February 1997—Larry Eugene Phillips and Emil Matasareanu engage LAPD officers with rifle fire after a botched bank robbery. Responding SWAT officers armed with rifles finally neutralize the two suspects at close range, but not without incurring casualties.

The typical police tactical rifle issued by most agencies is the AR-15, or one of its variants. There are others, of course, such as the Ruger Mini-14, the Steyr AUG, H&K's excellent 53 and 93, and some other imported rifles. Most of these are chambered in .223 caliber. This is no mere coincidence, as the .223 cartridge, although not perfect, offers great benefits to urban police officers. Although this is not specifically an AR-15 book, this weapon is featured prominently because of its widespread acceptance in police circles. However, the concepts presented apply equally to any other weapon.

The tactical rifle offers several advantages to the officer, including the following:

- The .223 rifle offers greater probability of stopping an armed suspect with a minimum number of rounds than the service pistol, submachine gun (SMG), or shotgun (at greater distances). "Minimum rounds equals minimum force." This is a very attractive concept in our litigious times. The terminal ballistics of the .223 rifle are not very powerful by rifle standards, and are certainly no guarantee, but they are dramatically better than the status quo.
- The .223 rifle defeats most types of body armor available and reduces the likelihood of a suspect's failure to stop after being hit. Additionally, most light cover is easily penetrated by the .223 round without excessive penetration. Moreover, missed shots, or projectiles that traverse suspects and exit tend to be less of a hazard to the local populace than pistol ammunition due to the design of the bullets.
- While, statistically speaking, officers employ the tactical rifle at much closer distances than is thought "traditional" for rifles, they can also employ it at distances far beyond what is reasonable for a pistol or a shotgun.

It is important that the tactical rifle team officer understand that the rifle is not intended to "firepower" a suspect into submission, nor is it intended as an ultra-long distance "sniper's" tool, although in a pinch, it can do those things. The goal of the tactical police rifleman is to fire only the minimum number of rounds necessary to solve the tactical problem at hand. Therefore, it is important to guarantee first-round hits and view *every round as a final exam.*

In an effort to guarantee his shots every time, without fail, the rifleman will seek to get as close to a threat as possible without tactically compromising himself or other officers. The average police marksman (sniper) engagement distance nationwide is less than 75 yards. The average rifle encounter worldwide (in both urban and rural scenarios) rarely exceeds 50 yards, with urban engagements coming closer to 25 yards. Moreover, police

The patrol/CQB rifle is not the same as a precision marksman's weapon.

Neither is the rifle a substitute for the other traditional police weapons, such as the pistol, shotgun, or submachine gun.

The rifle, when properly deployed, offers great advantages to the police offi-cer. One advantage is extreme precision at medium range, far in excess of any-thing else previously available to officers.

Although some agencies have been deploying rifles and carbines for many years, the concept is still new to the vast majority of urban law enforcers.

riflemen (tactical riflemen, not snipers) have rarely engaged outside 25 yards. One highly decorated and admired police officer and trainer in southern California works for an agency that has deployed carbines in special circumstances for quite some time. His most distant shot was *57 feet!*

The idea of deploying two blocks away and waiting for a shot is not realistic or tactically sound in an urban environment. We are not suggesting that you get close enough to poke the armed suspect with your gun muzzle, but simply to get within an engagement distance where you can insure exact precision. *Get as close as the tactical situation allows, get as steady as possible, and be able to guarantee the shot (if it is needed).*

There are three types of deployment for the tactical rifle in law enforcement, as follows:

- *Dynamic Confrontation*—This is the typical police gunfight scenario where a police officer confronts a suspect during a crime in progress, or where the officer is fired upon by the suspect(s) and must defend himself. These are fluid events with little or no command structure in place at the outset.
- *Static Containment*—This situation is often found when officers arrive on scene while the suspects are still there. Becoming aware of the police presence, the suspects change to a defensive or "siege" posture. The mission of these officers is to "lock down" the situation until specialized units such as negotiators and Special Weapons may respond.
- *Special Tactical Operations*—This is the SWAT deployment of tactical rifles for either containment or entry. Many teams are rethinking the type of entry weapon they need, and they are sometimes finding the typical MP5 submachine gun to be lacking. These operators take the rifle "inside" on a regular basis.

In a dynamic confrontation, the officer is responding to what he perceives. His actions are conceptually reactive in

In the search for the ideal police rifle, some have touted a lightweight bolt-action rifle as "the answer." Although such weapons may, in fact, be pressed into service in this role, they are not the best answer because of the diversity of mission requirements.

Others have opined that surplus military-type weapons, or older designs such as this Marlin 336, would do well in the police role. While this is true, they are not the best choice for departmental use unless financial resources are at a minimum.

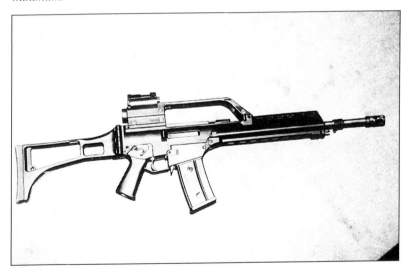

Space-age weapons such as this Heckler & Koch G36 offer many of the things essential to urban police officers, but oftentimes their expense limits the extent of their deployment. (Photo courtesy of Cory Trapp, SAS Products.)

The simplest answer, financially, logistically, educationally, socially, and even ballistically, is a version of the U.S. Military service rifle. This one is a Bushmaster Dissipator AR-15-type rifle with collapsible stock.

The most advanced . . . and expensive . . . rifle system available today is the HK G36. Is it really better than the other weapons available?

There are many weapons of foreign origin that suit the urban police officer just fine. This is the FN-FNC. This particular rifle was used in the popular motion picture that preceded (and some speculate may have inspired) the North Hollywood bank robbery.

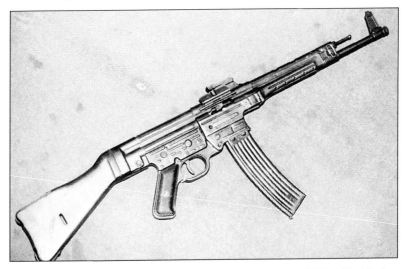

The urban rifle/assault rifle concept dates back to 1943 World War II with the innovative German concept of the storm gun. Chambered in the intermediate cartridge 7.92 Kurz, the Sturmgewehr StG-44 was the predecessor to virtually all of today's military rifles.

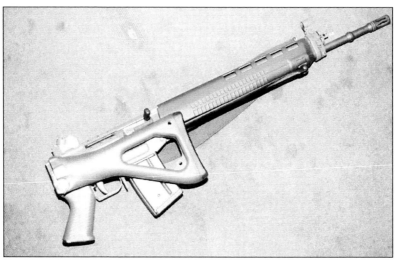

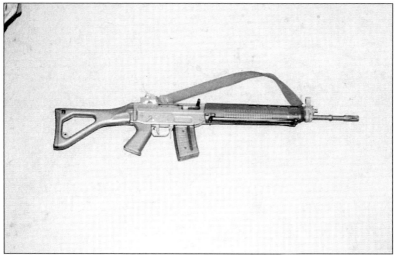

The SIG series rifles are ultra advanced in design and offer the officer many good features, but logistically they may not be the best choice for an American police department.

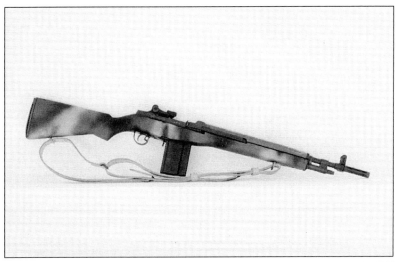

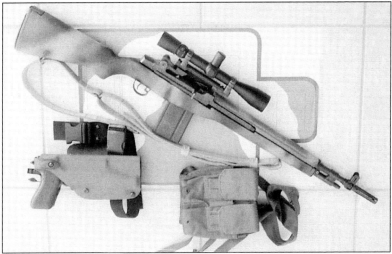

Although rifles chambered in .308/7.62 offer the rural officer many advantages over the smaller .223/5.56, they are too powerful and overpenetrative for urban CQB operations.

The ultra-modern Austrian Steyr AUG is another popular police rifle that exhibits many revolutionary features.

The Israeli-designed Galil rifle is a well-made version of the Kalashnikov. This rifle is imported into the United States, and it is also seen in southern Africa as the R4.

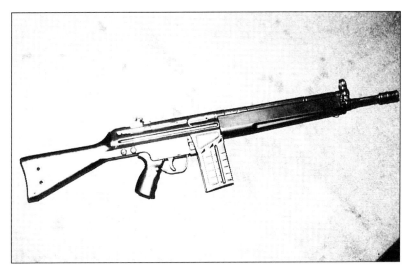

The HK-91/G3 in .308 is a fine and reliable rifle. It is also available in the preferable .223 caliber as the HK-93. (Photo courtesy of Cory Trapp, SAS Products.)

The Israeli Military Industries Micro-Galil is a strong contender in the police urban rifle field.

nature, and there is little time for planning. These are fluid, close-range, violent affairs of high intensity and short duration.

Static containment allows more time for planning a resolution, but not at the initial moments of deployment. Consider a scenario where, as the rifle-armed officer arrives on scene, the street has not been blocked off and both vehicular and pedestrian traffic are normally high. This situation demands a close-range deployment for fear that an uninvolved citizen will stumble into the line of fire. Moreover, a slightly elevated position is desirable in order to avoid line-of-fire problems.

Special tactical operations allow for the most planning. These are often highly planned and orchestrated operations with good intelligence on what the officers will be facing inside.

Each one of these situations would be best served with a specialized weapon, but a tactical rifle (suitably equipped and accessorized) will serve admirably in all three.

Firearms Safety and Dry Practice

1

For they had learned that true safety was to be found in long previous training, and not in eloquent exhortations uttered when they were going into action.
— Thucydides (404 B.C.)

Any discussion of the deployment of firearms must also include a discussion of safety. Firearms are inherently dangerous, and any careless handling may lead to embarrassment at best and tragedy at worst. With this in mind, we must establish rules and procedures for the daily handling of firearms that are intended to reduce such risk. The following safety rules are both simple and non-negotiable. They apply in training environments as well as in tactical situations.

- **Rule Number One: Treat All Guns as if They Were Loaded.** A firearm's utility comes from its loaded status, and, as such, that is the state in which most guns are found. Always assume that a firearm is loaded until you have determined otherwise.

- **Rule Number Two: Do Not Allow Your Muzzle to Cover Anything You Are Not Willing to Destroy.** This statement is self-explanatory, and it includes training situations as well as tactical environments. Many persons have been shot in training with supposedly "unloaded" guns. Don't take the chance.
- **Rule Number Three: Keep Your Finger Off the Trigger until You've Made a Conscious Decision to Shoot.** When moving in a tactical exercise, covering a threat, or handling the rifle in any manner, you must keep your finger clear of the trigger.
- **Rule Number Four: Be Sure of Your Target and What Is Beyond It.** Do not shoot at a sound or a shadow or at any unidentified suspect. Before you press the trigger, you must be absolutely certain that your target is an armed threat. Additionally, you must be aware of what is beyond the threat in the event of over-penetrative rounds or missed rounds.

These four rules are essential to safe gun handling. As police officers, we often become contemptuous of such rules because we handle firearms every day. But that is precisely why we must keep these rules in focus at all times.

The act of shooting is a motor skill. Motor skills are enhanced through repetitive practice. Within reason, the more you practice, the better shot you should be. This is not always the case, however, because it is unnatural to experience a small explosion mere inches from your face, as occurs during the act of shooting. As a result, we tend to flinch and anticipate the shot if we shoot excessive amounts of ammunition. This programmed response then surfaces during tactical operations, causing us to miss our targets.

There is a way to develop a high level of skill without firing a single shot. It is called dry practice. Dry practice is the effort a student puts forth off the range, at home, with an *unloaded* firearm. Dry practice allows you to execute perfect repetitions of all gun handling manipulations without the distracting muzzle blast or recoil. Remember that shooting is a motor skill, and that motor skills are enhanced through repetition. Dry practice allows you to perform an unlimited number of perfect repetitions. This will, in turn, yield impressive results at the range, as well as in stressful situations on the street.

Live fire is an important but minor part of the training. Each shot fired programs a subconscious imprint into the nervous system. If the shot is fired with perfect concentration and attention to basics, this is fine. If the shot is "thrown away," you've just programmed yourself to throw shots away. Look at live fire as a mere validation of your dry practice. The daily dry practice is the training; the occasional live-firing drill is the final exam. I have found that too much shooting actually makes officers poor shots.

There is a story about a man named Dave Westerhout. He was a member of the Rhodesian Defense Force during the unpleasantness in that country. The sociopolitical situation brought sanctions on his country, causing drastic shortages in ammunition. Ammunition is in short enough supply during a war, and with the sanctions exacerbating the problem, training ammunition was at an all-time low.

Westerhout instituted an experimental program of dry practice. He trained two groups—one with traditional and exclusive live fire and the other with dry practice. The results were surprising, yet educational for the tactical community at the time. When it came time for qualification, the dry-practice group shot higher scores than the live-fire group. This tells us that a high degree of skill is easily developed with dry-practice training.

The following procedure will help insure that no mishaps occur when you are dry practicing. Remember, guns are dangerous; treat them with respect.

1) Set a reasonable amount of time for the dry-practice drill. Certainly no more than 30 minutes at any one session is recommended. If you are tired or your concentration begins to lapse, it is time to stop.

2) Designate a dry-practice area that would contain a shot if one was inadvertently fired. All dry practice should be done there.

3) Unload the weapon, as well as all magazines, then chamber check the weapon to make doubly certain that it is, in fact, unloaded.

4) Place all ammunition in an area separate from the dry-practice area, such as in another room.

5) Place the dry-practice target (a business card will do fine) in such a manner that if a shot were inadvertently fired, the building material would contain the shot. Only display the dry practice target during the training session. As soon as the session is over, remove the target.

6) Mount the rifle into a ready position, point it in a safe direction, and recheck to make certain that it is, in fact, unloaded. Double-check all equipment to make sure no live ammunition is anywhere nearby.

7) You are now ready to concentrate fully on the dry-practice drills, which we will discuss later. Avoid all distractions. If you experience any distraction, go back to step 1 and begin the safety checklist again.

8) After completing the dry-practice session, immediately remove the dry-practice target. At this point, you may secure your firearm in the appropriate storage condition.

Some may think that this is a bit of nitpicking on my part, but I assure you that it is necessary from a liability, as well as a safety, perspective. More negligent shots are fired during routine gun handling and unorganized dry practice than at any other time. Don't let it happen to you.

Chamber Checking, Loading, and Unloading

2

In war we must always leave room for strokes of fortune and accidents that cannot be foreseen.

—Polybius, *Histories* (c. 125 B.C.)

These are the methods to use when handling rifles in training, as well as when loading and unloading them for tactical deployments.

CHAMBER CHECKING PROCEDURE

One often-neglected aspect of gun handling is the status check or chamber check. The chamber check has been called "one second of cheap insurance." By chamber checking you are making sure that your weapons are in the condition you want them to be in. This is applicable any time you handle a weapon. Even in a tactical situation, if you have the time to do so, it would be wise to make doubly sure you chambered a round than to be surprised by something unexpected.

To chamber check the AR-15 rifle, for example, you must first mount it into the low ready position with the muzzle pointed in a safe direction. Place the safety lever in its horizontal position, or ON SAFE. Note that if the weapon's trigger has been dry-pressed and the hammer is forward, the safety lever will not be able to be engaged. This is not an issue, but you must engage the safety as soon as the weapon is cocked.

Take the primary hand and engage the charging handle with the index finger and middle finger. Pinching the charging handle latch between the thumb and index finger, retract the charging handle approximately 2 inches. With the charging handle retracted, turn the weapon 90 degrees counterclockwise (ejection port up) and visually inspect the chamber. If you see a cartridge, it is loaded. If you do not see a cartridge, it is unloaded. In a low-light environment, where you cannot see a cartridge or you suspect that there may still be a cartridge chambered, you may use the support hand to check the chamber tactilely. To do so, simply bring the support hand back toward the receiver from its position on the fore-end and feel for that cartridge. Once you have verified the weapon's condition, allow the bolt to go back into battery, press the forward assist button to insure it is in battery, and engage the safety lever to ON SAFE. Finally, inspect the magazine to insure that it is in the condition you desire. Similar methods may be used for the different weapon systems.

The chamber check must precede any administrative gun handling maneuver, such as loading and unloading. Many mishaps occur at this juncture, so it is important for the officer to have a standard procedure for this function and follow it religiously.

LOADING PROCEDURE

The loading procedure begins at the low ready position. First, conduct a chamber check to ascertain the condition of the rifle. After verifying that the rifle is unloaded, insert a full magazine into the magazine well and seat it into place. Tug on the

An essential element of safety involves the chamber check, or status check, of the weapon. This is an administrative, not a tactical, operation and thus may be executed with the primary hand.

While maintaining the weapon in a ready position (safe muzzle direction), use the primary hand to locate the charging handle.

Move the charging handle to the rear, far enough to allow you to visually inspect the chamber.

If the light is so dim that visual inspection is impossible, you may use the small finger of the support hand to feel the partially chambered round.

When the chamber inspection is complete, allow the charging handle to move forward under the spring tension of the action spring.

If your weapon system is so equipped, lightly tap the bolt forward assist to insure that the bolt is fully seated.

magazine to be sure it is seated. Incidentally, for reliability reasons, it is recommended that 30-round magazines be loaded with only 28 rounds, and that 20-round magazines be loaded with only 18 rounds.

Having seated the magazine, take the support hand and grasp the charging handle on the support side of the rifle. Pull it to the rear as far as it will go, and allow it to go back into battery under spring tension. Do not "ride" the handle back into battery; rather, let go of it. Immediately resume the two-handed hold on the rifle. Now the weapon is loaded, but you must make certain. Conduct another chamber check to make sure.

UNLOADING PROCEDURE

As with the loading procedure, the unloading procedure begins with a chamber check. Step one is to remove the magazine and place it in a pocket. Making sure that the safety lever is ON SAFE, place the support hand at the ejection port and turn the rifle 90 degrees clockwise (ejection port down) at the waistline. Use the primary hand to slowly retract the charging handle. This will eject the chambered cartridge into the waiting hand. Secure the cartridge in a pocket. Resume the two-handed hold at the low ready, and conduct one final chamber check to be sure the rifle is unloaded.

* * * *

Remember, proper gun handling is an essential part of the Combat Triad (gunhandling, marksmanship, and mind-set) and is important to develop . . . if you want to win.

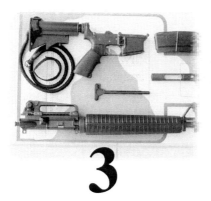

Care and Preventive Maintenance

3

Their science demands a great deal of courage and spirit, a solid genius, study, and consummate experience in all the arts of war.
— Marshall of France Sebastien de Vauban
A Manual of Siegecraft (1740)

A rifle, like any other man-made device, can fail. If the "device" is a weapon and is intended for hazardous duties, it will probably fail when it is least convenient for you! Much can be done at the operator's level to prevent this from happening, however.

One of the measures to insure reliability is selection of new factory-produced ammunition for actual deployments. Only a fool deploys with ammunition of unknown origin or of questionable reliability.

Likewise, careful observation and selection of magazines is important. The magazine (no they're NOT called "clips") is the heart of your semiauto rifle. Without a magazine, your weapon is a self-ejecting single-shot rifle! Inspect the carry magazines for minor cracks and for any dents or damage at the feed lips every day. I suggest to my students that they have two sets of magazines. The first set is intended for duty. These magazines are carefully maintained and cared for. The second set of magazines is for training only and never sees the street. This second set is used for speed reloads and malfunction training. It doesn't matter if these magazines are dropped or dirty, or even damaged.

As far as cleaning and maintaining the rifle itself, all the working parts of the rifle should be inspected and replaced if any damage is suspected. Normal cleaning after each training session will result in proper functioning of all parts of the weapon. A note about solvents and oils: every year someone invents new stuff and presents it as the final true answer for rifle maintenance. Be careful with your fighting tools, and avoid experimenting with new stuff. Let the competitive shooter or the hobbyist experiment for you. Lives will not be lost if a competitive or hunting rifle chokes on a new high-tech oil or solvent.

Following are the three solutions needed for rifle maintenance:

• A carbon solvent, such as Hoppe's No. 9 or Shooter's Choice. This cleans the carbon deposits from the rifle barrel itself.*
• An ammonia-based copper remover. This is used periodically to remove copper build-up in the bore. The two I've used with good results are Sweet's 7.62 Solvent and Shooter's Choice Copper Remover.*
• Break-Free to clean the remainder of the rifle, as well as to lubricate the moving parts.

* Used for the rifle barrel only.

Be careful about using products that strip every drop of lubricant from the metal of the rifle. These well-intentioned products should not be used on a regular basis because they tend to remove lubricant as well. The rifle is intended to be used with lubricant, not dry.

Along with the solutions listed above, you will need the following:

- Half a dozen bronze bore brushes (never use stainless-steel brushes).
- A one-piece bore cleaning rod.
- A bore guide (this keeps the rod centered in the bore and avoids any damage).
- A spear point jag (works better than the slotted variety).
- A big bag of patches matching the caliber (you'll use a lot of patches, so buy a lot). Some shooters will try to save a few bucks by reusing old patches. This is foolish for a fighting rifle. Patches are cheap compared to missing a criminal because your rifle has not been maintained properly.

The first step in the cleaning process is to unload the rifle (at least make sure it is unloaded). Next, follow the directions in the weapon's manual to disassemble it to its component parts.

I prefer to clean the chamber first, because that way, carbon dislodged during cleaning will not get into an already clean bore. The same goes for the inside of the receiver. There are chamber brushes specifically designed to clean the chambers on M16 rifles. These will also do fine for the HK, AUG, and other systems. Solvent is the solution for chamber cleaning.

To clean the barrel, attach a bronze brush to the one-piece cleaning rod. Wet the brush down with solvent. Using the bore guide, brush from chamber to muzzle and through the flash suppressor, using straight-through strokes. A good guideline is to use one stroke for every round you've fired, and wet the brush every five strokes. If you've put in an extensive training session and this much brushing is not feasible without overtime considerations, then just brush up to 50 times.

Remove the brush from the rod and replace it with the pointed jag. You can either wrap a cleaning patch around the jag, which is the preference, or you can pierce the patch in the center with the jag. Then wet it with solvent and run the jag

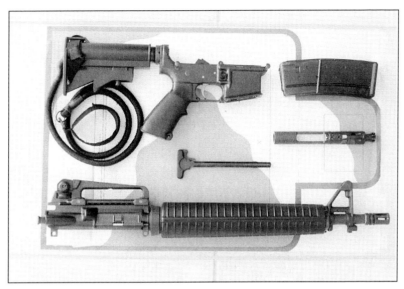

The M16/AR-15 in its field-stripped condition. The lower receiver assembly, the upper receiver assembly, the bolt carrier, the charging handle, and the magazine are visible.

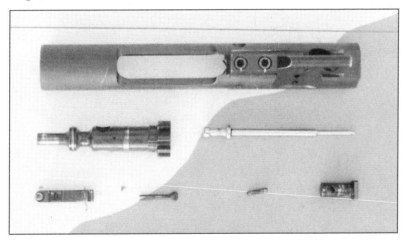

The bolt carrier assembly in a disassembled condition. Bolt carrier, bolt, extractor, extractor pin, firing pin, firing pin retaining pin, and cam pin.

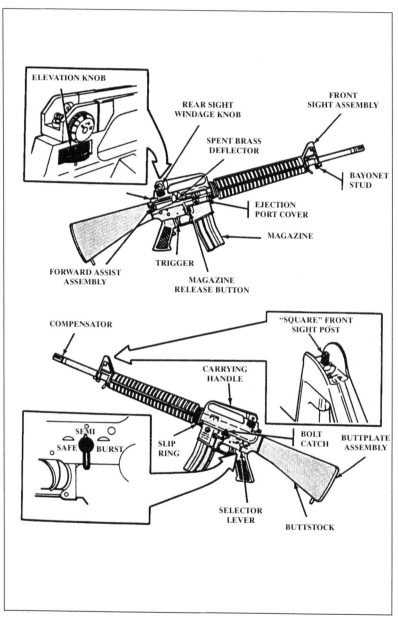

A page from the SMPD Tactical Rifle Manual *describing the nomenclature of the rifle.*

through out beyond the flash suppressor. Remove this patch (which should be very dirty indeed), replace it with a second wet patch, and repeat the process about five times. Now alternate wet and dry patches until the dry patches come out clean.

Take a clean patch and wet it with copper remover. Run the patch down the bore, back and forth a few times. Note that the copper is removed chemically, and not much "elbow grease" is needed. Let the copper remover sit in the bore for a few minutes.

Disassemble the bolt, again using the manufacturer's instructions. Clean every piece with cleaning solvent, such as Hoppe's, or with a cleaner/lubricant such as CLP or Break-Free; lightly lube; and reassemble. Some areas will have extensive carbon build-up and may require some meticulous brushing. Without getting into specifics for the different weapon systems, clean the receiver as much as possible with brushes and patches. After this is completed, lightly lube all the contact points and pivot points. Don't overdo this and end up with lube dripping off your rifle. Less is more.

Now, back to the bore. Run a clean dry patch through the bore. You will notice that it has a slight blue tint to it as it exits the bore. This is an indication that copper has been removed from the bore. Push a few more dry patches through to remove the final bits of copper-removing solution from the bore, and you are almost done.

Reassemble the rifle, and wipe the exterior with a clean rag. Wipe down the magazines as well. If the magazine has been in hostile weather conditions, it may be advisable to disassemble it for cleaning, but otherwise, leave it alone. Go through a function check to make certain everything is in working order, and the rifle is ready for storage.

The function check simply tests all the operating systems of the weapon. Cock the rifle, and set the selector lever on SAFE. Squeeze the trigger; the hammer should not fall. With the selector lever on SEMIAUTOMATIC, again squeeze the trigger. The hammer should fall. Holding the trigger to the rear, cock the rifle again. Now ease the trigger forward until the disconnector resets with a loud click. If your rifle is equipped with a three-round burst, or full auto, place the selector lever in that configuration. Squeeze the trigger; the hammer should fall. Holding the trigger to the rear, cock the rifle. Now release the trigger slowly. The disconnector should not have reset, thereby allowing fully automatic fire.

Many of the rifle systems in use today will function even when subjected to neglect and abuse. However, such treatment courts disaster. Proper care and maintenance will keep the weapon system ready to perform when you need it. As the old sarge used to say, "Take care of it, and it'll take care of you."

The Effects of Barrel Length on Terminal Ballistics

4

Battles are won by frightening the enemy. Fear is induced by inflicting death and wounds on him.

— Gen. George S. Patton Jr.

There have been many misconceptions about the .223 rifle round in law enforcement. One of these is that such a round is dramatically over-penetrative and likely to traverse several city blocks before stopping. Another myth is that rifles are the equivalent of a death-ray right out of *Star Wars*. Such notions tend to be exaggerated over time and often influence decision makers' choices when it comes to equipment selection and deployment. Few such rumors and legends are true.

My objective is to present an actual picture of what can be expected ballistically from the .223 round. I am not a scientist or a doctor, but there are many such men who've conducted vast amounts of research on the subject. I borrowed heavily from their work, as well as from that of military sources and police agencies such as the FBI.

What remained after all the material had been sorted out was a clear picture of the .223-caliber round and what a .223 rifle-armed police officer can expect from it. I've tried to present that picture here in a manner that laymen can understand.

There are three phases of ballistics study. The first is internal ballistics, which deals with what occurs from trigger press to the time when the round exits the muzzle. Next is external ballistics, dealing with the flight of the projectile and the environmental effects on that projectile. Finally, we have the study of terminal ballistics. This deals with what occurs when the projectile strikes its intended target and continues until its forward motion stops.

When a bullet traverses the body, it destroys tissue and blood vessels and may even break bones (depending on where it hits). This creates a permanent track, also called a permanent wound cavity. This wound cavity must be deep enough to reach the vital organs. This is the most important mechanism to cause wounding. Three different factors affect the severity of this wound.

When a rifle round is fired and the bullet is propelled down the bore, the bore's rifling imparts a gyroscopic spin to the bullet. This spin is required to stabilize the bullet during flight. This spin is not perfect, and most rifle rounds tend to yaw, or deviate slightly from a perfect point-forward position during flight. Note that this is *not* "tumbling" in flight. The portrayal of the .223 "tumbling" end over end is yet another myth. The .223 round does no such thing; it is known to yaw about 1 to 2 degrees, so that its long axis makes a slightly greater angle with the line of travel.

When the bullet strikes a body, this yaw causes a greater amount of tissue contact (or hard surface contact, if a barrier is hit) with the bullet. When these bullets strike the body, the yaw may be enhanced up to 180 degrees as they pass through tissue, sometimes ending up base forward.

Another factor affecting the severity of the wound is the ability of a projectile to expand. Expanding projectiles tend to damage more tissue by making a bigger hole. It is important, however, not to choose a round that expands too soon or too much, as this may mitigate penetration. Penetration is vastly more important than expansion when it comes to reaching the vital organs. If a bullet expands too quickly, it may never get to anything important.

The bullet's pointed shape makes it heavier at its base than at its point, so that its center of gravity at the rear of the bullet. When the bullet meets resistance, it attempts to rotate 180 degrees around its base to achieve a stable base-forward orientation. The stress of tissue resistance to the bullet's passage often overpowers the physical integrity of the bullet. This may cause the bullet to shed its jacket or bend at the cannelure (the point where it is crimped into the brass case), thereby enhancing the wound channel.

Finally, bullet fragments may come off the projectile itself and move radially away from the line of travel, in turn creating their own wound cavities. The .223 round creates a dramatically large permanent wound cavity due to these dynamics.

Another phenomenon that occurs, yet may not have far-reaching effects on the overall incapacitation of the subject, is the temporary wound cavity. When the projectile strikes the body, a temporary "stretch" of the muscles and organs will occur, much like the effect of an object thrown into a pool of water. Except for the brain, heart, and liver, most tissue will recover without much damage from the temporary-cavity effect.

Many individual officers, as well as agencies, have conducted numerous studies on the effectiveness of .223 bullets after striking intermediate barriers. The high-velocity .223 bullets lose much of their penetration potential after going through many common barriers, compared to pistol bullets, which tend to penetrate more.

In testing conducted by Bill Jeans and published in the National Tactical Officer's Association (NTOA) magazine, the only calibers that did not exit a "house" (as simulated for the test), were .223 softpoint and hollowpoint bullets. Moreover, the full-metal jacket (FMJ) M193 bullets showed no more penetration than the standard pistol bullets in service (9mm, .40 S&W, and .45 ACP).

Other testing conducted by the Snohomish County Sheriffs' Office showed that after exiting similar walls, the .223 bullets would only penetrate 5 1/2 inches of gelatin, compared to *nearly 20 inches for pistol bullets!* Apparently, when the .223 was shot through a wall, it began to break up and fragment, which reduced its penetrative characteristics.

The FBI has also conducted extensive testing on the 5.56mm/.223 round. They shot heavy clothing, steel plates, wallboard, plywood, light clothing, automobile glass, interior and exterior walls, as well as body armor. Their findings indicate the following: 1) soft body armor is no barrier against any .223 bullet; 2) with the exception of FMJ bullets, it is not a good idea to select the .223 for vehicular assaults as its penetration against automobile safety glass is generally poor, and only slightly better than on sheet metal; and 3) common barriers found in a residence, such as wallboard, plywood, or internal/external walls, are more easily penetrated by pistol calibers or large-bore rifle calibers such as the .308 (even in cases where such barriers have been penetrated, the wounding potential of the rounds is greatly reduced when compared to pistol calibers). These tests also indicate that the high-velocity .223 rounds may disintegrate if they strike an object that offers some resistance, such as concrete or brick. In such cases, since the bullets tend to break up, ricochets are generally less hazardous. This means that concerns about overpenetration and the danger to the populace presented by missed rounds have been greatly exaggerated, and that the 5.56mm/.223 is relatively safer than pistol bullets for everyone in the close-quarter-battle (CQB) application.

The U.S. Army Wound Ballistics Lab has conducted research on the ballistic effects of the M193 55-grain 5.56x45mm round (.223) and have determined that the large wound cavity produced by this round is largely the result of bullet fragmentation in the body.

Their studies show that if the bullet travels point forward, with no deviation, the wound track remains small. After about six inches of penetration, the bullet will yaw to approximately 90 degrees, flatten, and fracture at the cannelure. The flattened bullet nose remains in one piece and retains about 60 percent of the original bullet weight and penetrates about 13 inches in soft tissue. The rest of the bullet behind the cannelure shatters into many fragments that penetrate 2 to 3 inches radially away from the main wound track. These fragments cut their own path through the surrounding tissue, multiplying the total damage.

This is the description of the classic .223 wound. Such fragmentation is greatly dependent on the impact velocity of the projectile. If velocity is decreased, bullet fragmentation is reduced, as well as wound severity. As a basic guideline, rifles will exhibit this performance if impact velocity is at least 2,700 feet per second (fps). This means that such performance may be expected with 20-inch-barreled rifles out to 150 yards, and with 14- to 16-inch-barreled rifles out to 75 yards. If the impact velocity decreased to less than 2,700 fps (about 200 yards for the 20-inch barrel, and 150 yards for the 14- to 16-inch barrel), the bullet may break at the cannelure, but no fragmentation will occur. This will decrease the effectiveness of the round. Below 2,500 fps, i.e., beyond 200 yards for the 20-inch barrel, or 150 yards for the 14- to 16-inch barrel, there will not be any breakup, nor fragmentation, and the wound will not be as dramatic.

Based on these findings, you might be tempted to select a hollowpoint or softpoint round in order to enhance performance. That is not a good choice unless the muzzle velocities are drastically reduced (as in short-barrel weapons), as these projectiles have exhibited far less penetration in soft tissue than is required, due to early expansion and fragmentation. These projectiles deform rapidly on impact, and penetration may be as little as 6 inches with the lighter-weight bullets, such as the 40-grain variety. When these projectiles are fired from short-barreled (lower-muzzle-velocity) weapons, however, early or excessive fragmentation will be less than what is evident at higher velocities. Jacketed hollowpoint (JHP) or jacketed softpoint (JSP) bullets fired out of short-barreled rifles generally exhibit substantial deformation, occasional fragmentation, and some yaw. Penetration of the bullet is about 12 inches. This notwithstanding, the results are better than with the M885 or M193 in short-barreled rifles of less than 14.5 inches.

The most effective general-purpose ammunition for urban police tactical rifles with potential muzzle velocities above 2,500 fps (barrels of 14 inches or longer) is either the U.S. military M855 62-grain FMJ or the U.S. military M193 55-grain FMJ ammunition. The likelihood of fragmentation, not only in human adversaries but in building materials as well, enhances the potential for stopping the threat with minimal shots fired and reduces the danger to the surrounding populace if a round overpenetrates or misses the intended target. In weapons with muzzle velocity below 2,500 fps, such as the HK 53 or Colt Commando XM177, the M885 and M193 do not fragment or break up, which greatly reduces wound effect. A better choice for these short-barreled rifles would be one of the JHP or JSP bullets, which at least have some expansion potential and may enhance wounding.

The bottom line in terms of terminal ballistics, as well as the results of striking intermediate barriers, is that there are no guarantees. The .223 round is a marginal performer against humans. Although it offers certain advantages over handgun rounds or shotgun rounds, you must be careful to not expect too much. With a little information, however, you can go a long way in minimizing your liabilities (tactical, criminal, as well as civil and administrative) by selecting the right equipment, which includes the proper ammunition.

Shot Placement and Its Effects on Terminal Ballistics

5

The most important goal of our action is destruction of the enemy to the last limit of possibility.

—Field Marshall Prince Mikhail I. Kutuzov (1745–1813)

Although we discussed numerous studies and tests in the previous chapter with regard to the ballistic effects of the .223, the bottom line about the effectiveness of any caliber is that *there are no guarantees.* Centerfire rifle cartridges have a dramatically more damaging effect on human adversaries than, say, pistol rounds, but too many variables exist to be able to make predictions about their ability to stop an adversary with minimum force. One acquaintance of mine with extensive battlefield experience relates a story about an attack that they repelled with M16 rifle fire in Vietnam.

He said the firefight lasted into the early evening. In the fading light of a Southeast Asian sunset, they saw a small Vietcong (VC) soldier in the distance, running directly at their position, yelling and agitated. My friend, a fine shot, center-punched him with his M16. The soldier fell but momentarily got back up and resumed his charge. Several other shots hit him, but to no avail. Astonishment sharply turned to terror as they saw him more clearly. He was carrying a large satchel charge!

My friend told me that everyone, including the M60 gunner, opened up on this man. After several hits, including one from the M60 that hit his shoulder and literally ripped off his arm, he fell. This event disturbed everyone, because of the lack of effect their shots had, and the fact that the enemy had gotten danger-ously close with the satchel charge. No one slept that night.

The next morning, my friend went out onto the kill zone to see what had happened to the determined VC attacker. He found him, tangled in the wire, still alive! The man's arm had been shot off, and he had enough metal in him to sink a ship. He was still trying to set off the charge with his other hand but could not reach it! My startled associate finished him with a head shot from his 1911. A subsequent autopsy revealed *no drugs in the man's system.* If a man can take so much damage and still try to accomplish his mission, what will a single puny bullet do? *Remember, there are no guarantees!*

This is a sobering tale that illustrates very well why you should not put undue faith in firepower. This notwithstanding, there are things that you can do to stack the deck in your favor, in terms of the ballistic effect.

With the exception of a shot into the cranial vault, the likeli-hood of immediate incapacitation with a torso shot is difficult to predict. Humans—especially anesthetized or emotionally disturbed humans—are very durable. A wide variety of psy-chological, physical, and physiological factors exist, all of them affecting the final outcome. The only factors within the opera-tor's control are the placement of the shot via good marks-manship and the amount of tissue destroyed . . . hopefully via carefully selected ammunition.

There are two main methods of incapacitating a human adversary. A motivated opponent can only be stopped reliably and immediately by a shot that disrupts the brain or upper

COLD BORE SHOT   RANGE_____

The high sight line of the AR-15/M16 series demands holding high at close range. A head shot within 10 to 15 yards, for example, requires that the sight be held at the hairline in order to hit the cranio-ocular cavity. Using a standard point-of-aim/point-of-impact hold will result in a low hit at the jawline.

spinal cord. Other than the shot to the brain-housing group, the only other way to force incapacitation of the opponent is to cause circulatory collapse due to massive bleeding from shots to the heart, blood vessels, or major organs. The problem with the circulatory collapse method is that it takes time. Maybe enough time for him to kill you or another officer. There have been instances where suspects received nonsurvivable wounds and, although they would go on to die in the next few seconds, had not yet gotten the word. One notable example, if you recall, was the FBI gunfight in Miami some years ago. The rifle-armed suspect had been hit solidly with handgun fire and, although he received extreme ballistic trauma from FBI bullets, was still able to overwhelm the agents with his greater weaponry, killing several of them before he finally died from loss of blood.

Choose ammunition brands and loads that have been used successfully in the tactical field against real human opponents. Every year, new products come out promising to be "the answer." Well, that's fine, and we hope that they are good products, but a tactical situation is no place to be testing new ammo. Use what you know has worked in the past, and let someone else test the new stuff. And, of course, be ready in case even those rounds don't work.

Another very important aspect of increasing your chances of successfully ending a confrontation with the minimum force is shot placement. Some would tell you that a rifle bullet will cause so much damage that it matters not where you put it. This is foolish thinking. Granted, shots may be required to penetrate through intermediate barriers such as arm muscle. The ability to penetrate through to vital organs in these situations does not mitigate the need to place those rounds carefully. Repeat after me, Grasshopper: *Placement is paramount!*

The easiest part of an adversary to hit is the largest part, i.e., the upper body or the thoracic cavity. This can be roughly described as the area delineated from the top of the pectoral muscles to the solar plexus area in an inverted "U" shape. In this area are all the important organs and structures. Sure, a shot elsewhere, such as the abdomen, will cause the suspect to

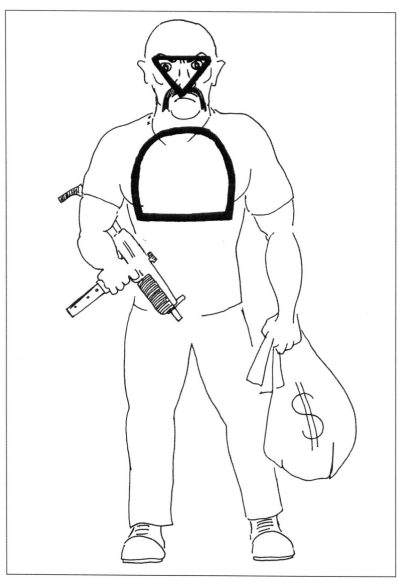

For best results, careful marksmanship to ensure shot placement is essential. Shots to the head area must be directed at the cranio-ocular cavity. This is best described by a triangle circumscribing the tip of the nose and the outside corners of the eyes. Chest shots must be directed at the thoracic cavity. This is best described as the upper chest area.

rethink his course of action, but it might not do so quickly enough to keep him from killing you.

Other times, if the body shots have not worked, or if there is an urgent need to stop the action due to hostages and so on, a shot to the brain may be required. The placement of this shot is also important because, even if you are shooting a rifle, the skull may deflect the projectile if it is not precisely placed.

Some of my colleagues in the training/tactical field have commented on the pelvic shot, or shot to the lower extremities in cases where a torso shot(s) has failed. They theorize than a man with a busted pelvis will not be able to do much. Not being a doctor, I spoke with an orthopedic specialist about the subject. He said that a demobilizing shot with any round would have to be in the hip joint itself. Although there are two joints, the target area is not much bigger than the proposed target area of the head. Inclusive with that is the difficulty in determining an exact aiming point to target those structures—especially on the move. He went on to explain that the pelvis itself is a ring structure, which means that it must fracture in two places to become unstable. Moreover, pelvic bones are very hard, and thus difficult to fracture. Yes, rifle rounds will do a better job than pistol rounds, but remember the stuff about "guarantees." The main point is that it is no easier to hit the pelvic hip joints than it is to hit the cranio-ocular cavity. So when in doubt, and if it is available, go for the head shot.

For the straight-on shot, the triangle-like target area is bordered by the outer tips of the eyebrows to the tip of the nose. This is called the cranio-ocular cavity. If you can, imagine a band stretching around the head, encompassing the ears and the area between the ears (as viewed from the back). This is called the parietal band, and it is where the brain shot should be placed if a straight-on shot is not available.

Some renowned medical ballisticians have said that a shot with a rifle anywhere in the brain vault will cause so much damage that it will shut off the entire machine. This may be true ... most of the time. I had an opportunity to talk with a retired FBI sniper with extensive practical experience. He said that in his experience, no hostage taker has ever been able to press the trigger when hit in the brain vault with a rifle-caliber bullet.

However, he told me of an incident in one of the Great Plains states where a man had taken a woman and baby hostage. He held the woman in front, with a revolver to her head, and kept the baby, in a backpack, strapped to his back. When the sniper saw him cock the revolver (approximately 2 pounds to discharge it), he knew that a hostage would be killed if he did not react. He shot the suspect in the right ear, at a descending angle of about 3 degrees, and dropped him. Everyone (mother, child, and criminal) fell down due to the pull of gravity on the shot suspect, but the hostage taker was not able to get his shot off. When the rescue team approached to pull the hostages to safety, they saw that the hostage taker was dead, but his trigger finger was still moving in a final attempt to press the shot. In other words, the message was being sent, but there was not enough electrical impulse from the command/control center (brain) to make it happen. Keep that in mind if ever called to make a head shot in a hostage situation.

Bullets are not particularly good at what they do. Rifle bullets are dramatically better than pistol bullets in their terminal ballistic effects, but they are not a perfect solution. In any case, be ready for the time when they do not work. If such a thing happens, be ready to hit the suspect again until he stops. This second shot may have to be to the cranio-ocular cavity.

Principles of Marksmanship

6

Make peace a time of training for war, and battle an exhibition of bravery.
—The Emperor Maurice, *The Strategikon* (c. A.D. 600)

Six factors comprise the basics of marksmanship. They are applicable to all forms of shooting, and if you observe them religiously, you will hit what you wish to hit. These principles are sight alignment, sight picture, breathing, trigger control, position, and follow-through. These principles must be observed in live-fire training as well as in dry practice.

SIGHT ALIGNMENT

Sight alignment is a condition where the very tip of the front sight post is centered, vertically and horizontally, in the rear sight aperture. This alignment is actually the relationship between the front sight, the rear sight, and the eye, regardless of the presence or absence of a target. The eye should be

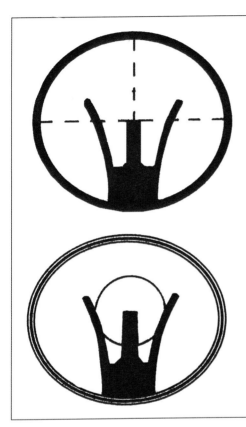

THE PROPER SIGHT ALIGNMENT: The top of the front post is centered in the rear aperture, with visual focus on the top of the front sight.

THE PROPER SIGHT PICTURE: The sight alignment is superimposed on the target, at the desired spot to be hit. The rear aperture and target are seen slightly out of focus, while the front sight is in perfect visual focus.

The proper use of the sights.

positioned approximately 2 to 6 inches away from the rear sight aperture (depending on the sights and the individual), looking through it at the front sight. The eye will automatically center the front sight post in the rear aperture if the visual focus is on the tip of the front sight.

SIGHT PICTURE

Sight picture is the correct sight alignment discussed in the previous paragraph, superimposed on the center mass of the target. To form a sight picture, the shooter is dealing with three points in space: the rear sight, the front sight, and the target. The

Proper cheek placement (aka stock weld) and eye relief are essential elements of any shooting position. Proper technique will allow consistent sight picture.

human eye can only focus on one point at any given time. In order to maintain all three points in relative alignment, the shooter must focus on the front sight and see it with crystal clarity. He will still see the target and the rear sight well enough, although somewhat out of focus, to keep all three points aligned. In order to sustain visual focus on the front sight, the shooter must close his support-side eye.

Notice that an armed suspect does not have a specific "aiming point" emblazoned on his chest, like the traditional bull's-eye zeroing target. A proper sight picture involves placing the sights on the center mass of the visible target. If an optical sight, or scope, is used, the process is greatly simplified. The operator looks through the scope and sees the reticle and target on the same visual focal plane. He places his visual focus on the reticle center for a proper sight picture.

BREATHING

Having attained a correct sight picture, the shooter must now control his breathing. If the shooter tries to shoot while

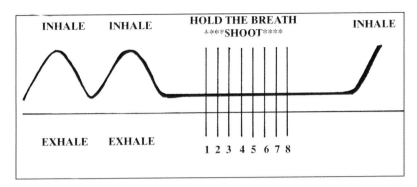

The most easily employed breathing cycle involves the concept of the empty lung. Exhale the last breath and begin the firing process. You will have approximately eight seconds to make the shot before the oxygen debt begins to affect you.

breathing, the rising and falling of the chest muscles will cause the shot to go errant. The normal respiratory cycle lasts about four to five seconds, with a natural pause of two to three seconds between cycles. During the natural pause, the breathing muscles are relaxed and still. As a result, the rifle will not move during this pause. The shot should be fired at this time. The process is as follows; breathe in, breathe out, pause – shoot – pause, breathe in, breathe out.

It is important for the shooter to fire his shot within eight seconds of the beginning of the respiratory pause. To go longer causes blurred vision and the inability to focus clearly on the front sight because the oxygen level in the brain is depleting. If a shot is not fired within the eight-second time window, begin another breathing cycle.

TRIGGER CONTROL

Trigger control is the manipulation of the trigger in a manner that does not disturb the existing sight picture. This is the most crucial element of marksmanship. Proper trigger control consists of a smooth and steady application of pressure to the trigger straight to the rear, until, at some point, it suffices to make the rifle discharge a shot. It is important that the actual shot come as a surprise to the shooter. The shooter will know that he will shortly be firing a shot, but he does not know the exact, specific instant that it will discharge. If the shot is specifically anticipated, the shooter will involuntarily flinch, or bear down on the weapon in anticipation, and cause the shot to go errant.

Pressing the trigger may be compared to using an eyedropper from which a single drop is wanted. The process is to align the eyedropper with the eye, focus on the tip of the eyedropper, and c-a-r-e-f-u-l-l-y apply constantly increasing pressure until a drop forms and falls into the eye, by surprise. If you anticipate the drop, or try to force it, you will get eye drops all over your face rather than in the target (the eye).

In some of the less stable positions, the sights will move in relation to the target, although they may be in perfect alignment. In such situations, the shooter must employ an interrupted trigger press. This is done by commencing the trigger press as usual. When the sights begin to drift away from the desired point, hold the trigger press. Do not release the pressure. When the sights are again on target, resume the pressure. Continue with this until the weapon discharges.

The manner in which you grip the rifle is also important in terms of your ability to control the trigger. With weapons equipped with a pistol grip, such as the AR-15, the primary hand is placed as high as possible on the pistol grip of the rifle. The primary hand's thumb is placed on top of the safety lever, prepared to disengage it. The trigger finger is held straight until the decision is made to fire. At this point, it touches the trigger at the first pad of the finger. The power of the grip comes from the last three fingers.

Now as far as the speed of the shots are concerned, this is determined by the precision required for each shot. This in turn is dictated by the actual size of the available target. A close-range target, say a chest shot across the room, requires little precision. The same suspect's head as he looks from behind his hostage, or if he is alone at 100 yards, requires much greater precision in sighting and trigger control.

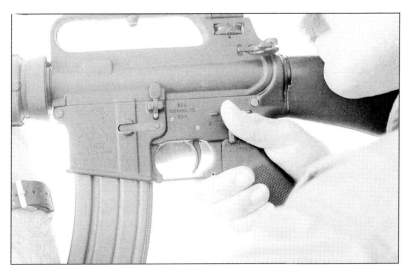

Grasping the pistol grip or pistol grip area of the stock with a high grip allows easy operation of the safety lever and promotes trigger control.

Trigger finger placement should allow you to press the trigger to the rear with smooth and even pressure. The exact placement for greatest efficiency calls for the first pad of the finger to be in contact with the trigger.

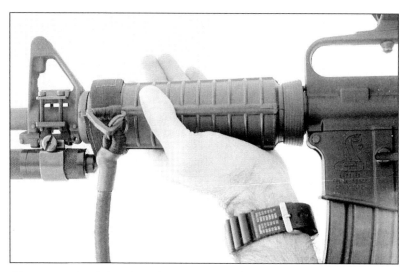

The support hand does just what its name implies: it "supports" rather than grips the fore-end of the rifle.

POSITION

Position is the platform upon which the weapon is held and from which it is fired. All firing positions have four elements in common. These are bone support, muscular relaxation, natural point of aim, and stock weld.

Bone support means that the weight of the rifle is supported by skeletal structure and not by muscular strength alone. The mechanics of each position must be learned and developed to enhance bone support and minimize muscular involvement.

Muscular relaxation means, specifically, that once in position the shooter must relax his muscles. With bone support and muscular relaxation, the rifle will remain aligned on the target without any effort or muscular control from the shooter.

Natural point of aim is adjusting the position so that when the shooter relaxes and the weapon is fully supported, the sights are aligned on the target without any effort from the shooter. To find the natural point of aim, get into position and aim the rifle. Now close your eyes and relax. After a few seconds, open your eyes and verify that you are still on target. If the rifle's alignment on target has moved, align the entire position until the rifle is back on target.

Stock weld is the consistent placement of the shooter's cheek onto the rifle stock at the very same spot every time, and from shot to shot. Stock weld is crucial because it determines the eye relief, which in turn affects the sight picture. Select a comfortable (with consideration to eye relief) spot on the stock and remember to locate your cheek at that spot every time you mount the rifle. Placing a small piece of tape at that spot may assist you in remembering the spot until it becomes reflexive.

FOLLOW-THROUGH

Follow-through is maintaining attention on the fundamentals and controlling the rifle and the trigger after the shot has been fired. This is to prevent disturbing the alignment before the shot has left the bore. To "follow through," a shooter maintains his position and holds the trigger back during recoil. He resumes his sight picture as soon as his weapon recovers from recoil. At this point he releases the trigger far enough to reset the disconnector (this will be an audible "click" as the trigger begins to travel forward again). As soon as the trigger is reset, he is ready to fire again if the situation calls for it.

PUTTING IT ALL TOGETHER

The sequence of events begins with the eyes on target. The shooter mounts his rifle in whichever position the tactical situation calls for, with eyes on target. As the rifle is mounted, the shooter looks through the rear aperture to the front sight and aligns it with the center mass of the target. His finger is on the trigger, and he focuses on the front sight. Carefully, he begins to press the trigger, controlling his breathing, until the pressure suffices and a shot is fired.

After the shot is fired the shooter does not relax. He must follow through for an instant to make sure his shot was on tar-

All the essential elements of a firing position insures that the shots are placed with surgical exactness within the limits of the weapon system. Along with the basics of marksmanship, a good position is paramount to field accuracy.

A good position exemplified—bone support, muscular relaxation, natural point of aim, and stock weld.

get. The rifle is then lowered to the low ready position and the shooter looks for his target and its reaction or lack of reaction. He assesses the target for a moment to insure that it has been hit solidly and is (theoretically) no longer a threat. If the threat remains, he deals with it. Then he must scan left and right to look for other threats (there may be more). This is called the after-action assessment, and it must be done in tactical situations as well as in training. This will condition the officer to maintain alertness and not relax too soon.

Threats within 20 to 25 yards should be engaged with controlled pairs (two immediate and controlled shots), unless a single precise shot is required, such as in a hostage incident. Threats beyond 25 yards should be engaged with single precise shots.

Iron Sights and Optics

7

The rifle will probably break before the scope does.
—Anonymous Navy SEAL
Speaking of the Advanced Combat Optical Gunsight (ACOG) scope

The various sighting systems allow the operator to orient his weapon, visually, on the target. Unless you are so close that you can literally poke the suspect with the gun muzzle, all shots require the use of the sights. Think of the sights as a guidance system for the shot. There are two types of sighting systems: iron sights and optical or scope sights.

There are various types of iron sights, but the one most often seen on service rifles is the aperture sight as found on the M16, H&K, and others. The aperture sight offers wide field of view, speed, and durability. The aperture sight is designed to be looked through, not at. An operator looks at the front sight through the rear sight aperture. He can simply ignore the rear sight, since the eye will normally center the front post in the rear aperture. All that remains is to orient the sight picture on the target, focus on the front sight, and fire. Designed for the battlefield, iron sights are rugged. They are not affected by inclement weather conditions, and they rarely lose their zero due to rough handling. And they are not an additional expense, since most fighting rifles are issued with sights.

Optical or scope sights offer many advantages over iron sights, but not without some liabilities. The liabilities may include fragility of the scope, larger overall size of the weapon, and overly high sight line. Some ultra-modern rifles, such as the Steyr AUG, are issued with optical sights. These optical sights can either be magnifying devices that allow closer inspection of the target or simple, nonmagnifying aiming devices. In years past, optical sights were contraindicated on a fighting rifle due to the fragility of the devices. This is not the case anymore, as there are several extremely rugged scope sights that may very well be more robust than the rifles they are attached to. Make no mistake, these scopes are not cheap, but they are, in my opinion, worth it. The optical or scope sight has advantages over iron sights that may make the difference in low light, in situations where the visibility of iron sights is diminished or where visual identification of a small, obscured target is desired.

The target and aiming device are seen on the same visual plane, thereby simplifying the aiming process. This is a very considerable factor if teaching brand new riflemen to shoot. There are scopes, such as the Trijicon series, that have tritium illuminated reticles ("cross hairs," for you barbarians out there), allowing the operator to aim in low-light environments. Even without the tritium reticles, scopes tend to allow good visibility beyond what is possible with unaided vision in reduced light.

Care must be exercised when selecting a scope for a tactical (nonsniper) rifle. Keep the scope and mounting system as small and compact as possible. Keep the power (or magnification) level no higher than 4X. Ruggedness is paramount, since a tactical rifle is not going to be pampered like a sniper's rifle will be. This almost requires selecting a military spec scope and avoiding the hunting grade variety.

With the foregoing in mind, know that optical sights will

For best efficiency in the urban role, where every round must be accounted for, a lightweight, low-powered optical sight, such as this Trijicon ACOG, is a very good idea.

The front sight of most military weapons is protected with surrounding structures as on this Colt M-4 rifle.

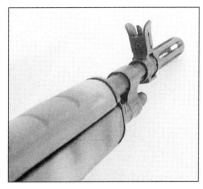

The protected front sight of an M1A/M14.

The protected front sight of an FNC rifle.

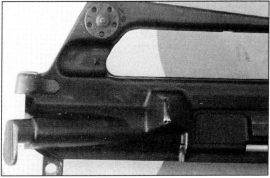

The protected front sight ring of a Swiss SIG 550 rifle.

The M16-A1 sight is not as adjustable but it is more robust.

The M16-A2 sight allows for ease of adjustments in the rear sight. For best efficiency, however, set the zero at the front sight and leave the rear sight at its lowest setting.

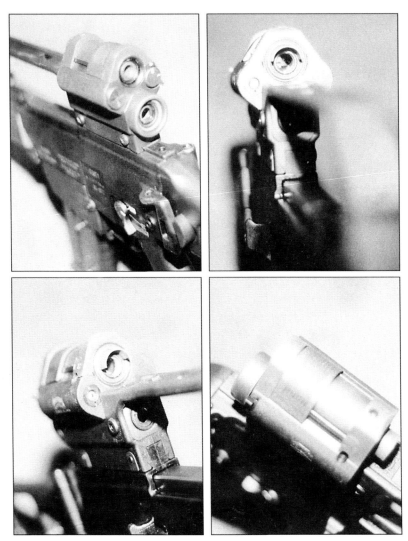

The high-tech optical sight of an HK G36 rifle.

enhance your operational capabilities. I equipped my personal
rifle and my team rifles with optical sights. The scope I selected
for my team, as well as for my personal rifle, was the Trijicon
ACOG series. The ACOGs have many advantages over other

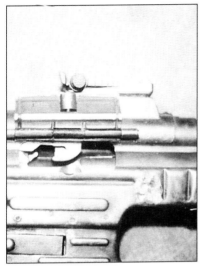 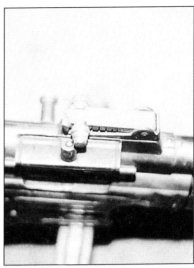

The rear sight of the first known "assault rifle," the German Sturmgewehr StG-44. This is a tangent-type sight often found today on Kalashnikov rifles.

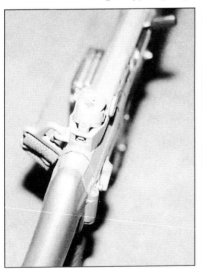 

The rear sight on the SIG 550 rifle is very similar in concept to the older HK 91 and 53/93 series rifles.

The front sight of the StG-44 was elevated above the bore, as are the sights of many of today's military and police rifles.

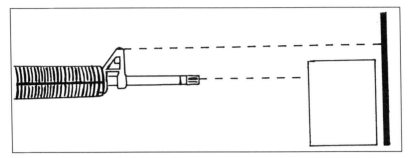

The elevated front sight must always be kept in mind to ensure surgical accuracy as well as to avoid striking cover.

A clearly visible front sight that's also protected is essential for a tactical rifle.

scopes. They are internally adjustable and feature a tritium-illuminated reticle for low-light use (during daylight use, the reticle appears black). Some of the scopes feature fiber-optic systems allowing the reticle to "glow" during daylight hours and tritium for use in low light. The scope housings are made of 7075-T6 aircraft aluminum alloy. This is the same stuff the M16 receivers are made of. In fact, the ACOG scopes are hard-anodized finished to match the receivers of the M16 rifle. Additionally, many of the reticle designs available have range-finding features. When zeroed at 100 yards, the range-finding reticle allows you to hold and shoot at varying distances out to 800 yards. The scope design uses aerospace seals to make the ACOG one of the most rugged scopes around, not to mention the fact that it is virtually waterproof.

Other optical sights of note, which have been used successfully, are the Aimpoint Comp M-III electronic dot sights. I have spoken to a number of operators who've used the Aimpoint in combat, and all have good reports. The Comp M-III has a three-minute dot. This means that the dot covers approximately 3 inches on the target at 100 yards. The dot intensity has nine settings for varying light conditions. The three-minute dot seems to be very versatile over a wider range of deployment scenarios than the older five-minute dot formerly available on the unit. This scope was designed for military units and is as rugged as anyone can expect it to be. One operator dropped his rifle from a moving vehicle during a training exercise. An immediate test at the firing range proved that the zero remained true and the scope was not damaged. The Comp M-III is also water-resistant.

The only negative aspect of the Comp M-III is the requirement for batteries. The issued batteries will last a very long time, but having a couple of extras on board is a good idea, just in case.

This sight may be mounted in such a way as to incorporate the use of a hand-held monocular night vision device (NVD). In this application, the Comp M-III is mounted well forward, as in the Scout Scope method, and the NVD is mounted directly behind the CompM-III. This system works extremely well.

Remember the purpose and mission of the tactical rifle. Precision at close distance is easier to attain with an optically sighted rifle. Efficiency in reduced light is also better provided with optical sights. Study the realities of your projected deployments and decide whether an optical sight is a good thing for your rifle. If it is, then buy the best. You are far better off with iron sights than with a substandard, cheaper-than-dirt scope. As with most tactical issues, there is no perfect solution. Pick the best tool for the job based on a realistic assessment of your mission needs.

Zeroing and External Ballistics

8

An improperly zeroed rifle is like an automobile without a steering wheel.
— Anonymous

The first part of this chapter is a recommended zeroing process for the tactical rifle. The AR-15-type rifle is used as an example because of its widespread acceptance in American law enforcement, but the concepts are applicable to the other rifles, keeping in mind the idiosyncrasies of their sighting systems.

First we must discuss the concepts of offset and holdover. *Offset* is the relationship between the line of sight using the sights and the centerline of the bore. The AR-15 has a high sight line, which is offset from the bore by 2.5 inches. *Holdover* is the difference between the point of aim and the actual strike of the bullet (point of impact). Holdover is based on the amount of offset designed into the particular rifle (2.5 inches for the AR-15; 3.0 to 3.5

inches if scope mounted), the trajectory of the round, and the zero of the rifle.

The zero of the rifle is determined by the shooter when sighting in, or "zeroing," the rifle. For most cartridges sighted at 100 yards or more, the bullet's trajectory will coincide with the line of sight at two points: one close (near zero) and one at the designated zero distance (far zero). The points of coincidence are determined by the "flatness" of the trajectory. The .223-caliber has a very flat trajectory. For example, if a .223-caliber rifle has been zeroed at 100 yards, this means the rifle will hit point of aim coinciding with point of impact at exactly 100 yards and maintain that flatness of trajectory from approximately 50 yards to approximately 200 yards. The point of impact will be slightly high or low at all other distances. Some agencies require that tactical rifles be zeroed at 50 yards to reflect realistic engagement distances. This is a good idea for iron sights. If equipped with optics, the rifle may be zeroed at 100 yards. This way, the officer need only hold "point of aim-point of impact" for all likely engagement distances, except for extremely close shots. At the end of this chapter there is a ballistics chart depicting the trajectory of typical .223 rounds.

Close-in shots to small targets, or to partially exposed targets (such as those faced when an armed suspect is wearing body armor) will require pinpoint accuracy. Such shots are much easier to guarantee when taken within 25 to 30 yards. Those shots, at that range, will routinely require that the officer raise his point of aim approximately 1.5 to 2.5 inches above his target spot in order to hit the exact spot he desires to hit. This is a result of the high sight line. Shots between this distance and 100 yards need not be compensated for because of the flat trajectory of the .223 round. The officer may simply hold center and expect center mass hits within 3 inches of the point of aim. Moreover, such long-distance shots to small targets are rarely required in a police rifle deployment.

The AR-15 is equipped with adjustable front and rear sights. Once the rifle is zeroed, the sights must not be touched or readjusted. The A2 sight has a large aperture, which is actu-

The zeroing process is essential. It involves firing a series of shots and adjusting the sights so that the strike coincides with the position of the sights. In this photo the author gives a police officer advice on his zero.

Establishing a solid firing position is paramount during the zeroing process and may even dictate the use of a bench rest to steady the weapon.

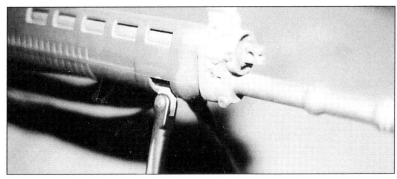

Care must be exercised on rifles equipped with bipods because the point of aim may change when the rifle is used in a position where the bipod is not deployed.

On the M16 series rifles, be certain that you zero using the smaller aperture.

The larger aperture may be used later at close quarters without a change in point of impact.

All adjustments should be made on the front sight for best results.

ally the "low light aperture." It allows for quick target acquisition and a better field of view. The smaller aperture is designed for long-range shooting in excess of 200 yards. All zeroing should be accomplished utilizing the small aperture. We've found that if an operator zeroes with the large aperture and then switches to the smaller aperture, his shots will be drastically high. However, zeroing with the small aperture and switching to the large one will not present the same problem.

To zero the AR-15 tactical rifle with the A2 sight, set the rear sight elevation drum to "8/3" (or "6/3" on short-barrel rifles) using the small aperture. Begin by shooting a 3-shot group from a supported (bench and sandbag) position at 25 yards. *Adjust the front sight ONLY.* Do not adjust elevation at the rear sight. The A2 rear sight is easily adjusted (and easily misadjusted) and inherently fragile. Making adjustments at the front sight with the rear sight held at its lowest position optimizes your chances of not losing zero in storage or transport. This procedure at 25 yards will get the rifle's shots "on paper" quickly.

Rifles equipped with the A1-type round front sight post have adjustments of 1 inch per click at 100 yards (1/2 inch at 50 yards, 1/4 inch at 25 yards) if equipped with 20-inch barrels. If they are equipped with 16-inch barrels, the adjustments are 1 1/4 inch per click at 100 yards (5/8 inch at 50 yards, 5/16 inch at 25 yards).

Rifles equipped with the A2-type square front sight post have adjustments of 1 1/5 inch at 100 yards (3/4 inch at 50 yards, and 3/8 inch at 25 yards) when fitted with 20-inch barrels. Rifles with the 16-inch barrel have adjustments of 2 inches at 100 yards (1 inch at 50 yards, and 1/2 inch at 25 yards). Regardless of which front sight configuration is present, the rear sight may be adjusted for windage via the windage adjustment knob on the right side of the rear sight assembly. The windage adjustments are 20-inch barrel 1 click = 0.3 cm at 25 yards, 16-inch barrel 1 click = 0.5 cm at 25 yards.

The initial zero of the rifle must be at 25 yards from prone on a sandbag, or off a bench, to get the shots on the paper. Adjust the front sight with the rear sight set at 8/3. This will eliminate the need to *ever* have to change a sight setting in tactical environments. Fire a three-shot group and make note of its center. Now adjust as needed to hit center. Verify with subsequent three-shot groups.

Once the rifle has been roughly zeroed at 25 yards and is hitting center, refine the zero at 50 yards or 100 yards, depending on perceived need. This should be relatively easy to do with a preliminary zero at 25 yards. It is important to shoot the rifle at all likely distances, from 7 yards out to and slightly beyond 200 yards, to become familiar with the trajectory characteristics of the rifle and ammunition. With a 50- to 100-meter zero, the officer need not hold over or hold under for the vast majority of tactical engagement. The center hold will yield hits roughly within a 3-inch radius of the point of aim at all realistic distances except for very close.

The following table depicts bullet drop at various distances for a .223-caliber AR-15 zeroed at 50 yards with standard GI ball ammo at approximately 3,000 fps. These are computer-generated approximations only, and the officer should develop his own data with his own rifle and ammunition. This table is included to illustrate the foregoing points. The 50-yard zero is suggested for urban close-range deployments.

There are three distances at question with the tactical rifle. The first one is from close quarters out to approximately 20 yards. This may require rapid response activity, such as during an officer rescue or tactical entry. Regardless of zero (25 yards, 50 yards, 100 yards, or more), the round will tend to impact

BULLET DROP AT VARIOUS DISTANCES
FOR A .223-CALIBER AR-15 ZEROED AT 50 YARDS
WITH STANDARD GI BALL AMMO AT
APPROXIMATELY 3,000 FPS

0 yards	-2.5"	120 yards	+1.6"
10 yards	-1.9"	130 yards	+1.7"
20 yards	-1.4"	140 yards	+1.8"
30 yards	-0.9"	150 yards	+1.7"
40 yards	-0.4"	160 yards	+1.6"
50 yards	0.0"	170 yards	+1.5"
60 yards	0.4"	180 yards	+1.3"
70 yards	0.7"	190 yards	+1.0"
80 yards	+1.0"	200 yards	+0.7"
90 yards	+1.2"	210 yards	+0.3"
100 yards	+1.4"	220 yards	- 0.1"
110 yards	+1.5"	230 yards	-1.8"

about 1 1/2 to 2 1/2 inches low because of the AR-15's high sight line. This is not an issue for center-mass shots, as the officer need only hold center and expect a good hit. For small targets at close range (i.e., head shots), such as would be faced with a partially ensconced, or armored, suspect, the officer must *always hold slightly high.*

The next distance involves shots at the more statistically likely engagement distances of 20 to 50 yards. Ideally, the trajectory of the round will become "0.0" within that distance interval, so that the officer may hold center for all engagements and still expect a center hit. The variance, throughout the interval, should not rise or fall more than 3 inches.

The final distance involves the "outer edge" of urban engagement, beyond 100 yards. The possibility, statistically speaking, of such a long shot being required in a city is very slight. However, should the need arise, a 50-yard zero will maintain a maximum variance of no more than 2 inches high or low out to 250 yards!

Administratively, executing the cold shot, as well as the five-shot group, during training sessions is more efficient at 50 yards than at any other distance.

A note of suggestion: When you have zeroed the rear sight for windage, it is advisable to paint index marks on its face corresponding with index marks on the receiver to make sure at a glance if it has been moved.

Again, you can use the same process to zero other rifles, paying attention to the mechanics of their inherent sighting systems. The process is identical for optically sighted rifles, except, of course, for the adjustments that are made on the scope's knobs. You may choose to zero at any distance, but be certain to keep in mind the real distances expected in encounters.

Carry and Ready Positions

9

I am not a bit anxious about my battles. If I am anxious, I don't fight them. I wait until I am ready.
— Field Marshal Viscount Montgomery of Alamein (1887–1976)

There are various methods for carrying the tactical rifle. They are all based on the officer's perception of threat. The carry/ready positions have one predominant point in common, and that is muzzle control. The officer must always be conscious of the direction of his muzzle and avoid "covering" other officers or citizens inadvertently. Whether the rifle is carried muzzle up or muzzle down is not important. In some tactical situations, the high ready, or high muzzle, will be used to cover second story threats or to prevent the muzzle from catching on debris or vegetation. In other situations, the low ready will be more useful.

There are a few other positions of note. For times when there is no obvious expectation of threat and ease of movement is the only consideration, the old military port arms (muzzle high) will allow the operator to move quickly from point to point without the risk of catching the rifle on any obstacles. Other times, when the muzzle must be kept low, the low inside ready, which places the shouldered rifle's muzzle by the support-side leg, will provide good service.

Part of professionalism is the way we handle our weapons. We have all seen news footage of (and perhaps witnessed in person) officers carrying their long guns (shotguns, rifles, or submachine guns) like backwoods hunters on the way home from a squirrel hunt. Oftentimes, the weapons are dangling at their sides from their hands, waving to and fro, covering everyone's feet. Other times, these weapons are seen balanced precariously on an officer's shoulder, almost smacking bystanders nearby with the barrel every time the officer turns (à la, *The Three Stooges*). Particularly unprofessional is using the rear sight base on the AR-15 rifle, aka "carry handle," to, well, carry the rifle like a latté-swilling yuppie on his way to a board meeting. Such poor and unprofessional weapons handling is unacceptable.

RANGE OR ADMINISTRATIVE CARRY

At the firing range, or any other training session and/or environment, the rifle should be in one of three positions. The rifle will be in a *ready position* or *on target* while on the line, at the instructor's direction. At any other time it will be *slung* muzzle down on the support side or tactically across the chest with the muzzle down.

Sometimes during training, it may be necessary for the instructor to interrupt a firing drill in order to provide further instruction. At such times, complete unloading may be impractical. His directions will be to "put them *on safe* and *let them hang*." This indicates engaging the safety and allowing the weapon to hang in front of you, muzzle down, by the sling. While the instructor is in front of the line, do not touch the weapon with your hands.

Muzzle down/support-side carry (aka "African carry"). Note the support hand controlling the muzzle.

To present the rifle, pivot the support hand toward the threat, simultaneously reaching underneath the weapon with the primary hand to obtain the trigger group.

Roll the rifle off the shoulder and . . .

. . . on target!

The African carry/muzzle down support side carry.

The tactical sling carry. The sling shown is a bungee sling.

The tactical sling should allow a proper ready position, as well as a proper firing position.

If the class/instructor is working with a two-relay system, i.e., one group on the line and a second group behind the line loading magazines and so on, *do not handle the rifles while others are in front of the line. Get used to moving and working with the rifles slung, and do not set them down. Get accustomed to having the rifle on your person at all times during a training session.*

TACTICAL SLING-ARMS

The rifle should be deployed with a tactical sling. This sling differs from the standard type of sling in that the tactical sling allows the rifle to hang directly in front of the officer's body. This sling must be configured so that it is long enough to allow the officer to mount the weapon easily. This may involve looping it over the neck only, or over the neck and support arm. The advantage of utilizing the sling is that the officer has full control of the rifle at all times, since it is, in fact, attached to his body. If he needs a free hand, or both hands free, he need not place the rifle down on the ground or precariously balance it against something. The sling will also become quite useful in terms of tactics.

READY POSITIONS

When you are operating in a training environment or a tactical environment (as specifically different from the administrative setting), the following ready positions will be of great utility, as they allow for carry of the rifle while enabling a quick response to threats.

High Ready

The *high ready* was developed by John Satterwhite, a shotgun master and exhibition shooter. Some trainers dismiss the high ready as useless, since it came from the exhibition/competitive arena. I believe that they are foolish to do so, because the high ready is appropriate for some tactical situations. The one disadvantage is that the high muzzle may obscure threats below

The high ready position (note trigger finger position).

The high ready involves keeping the eyes, muzzle, and potential target in line with each other. It is also useful for covering second-story threats from above.

the line of sight. However, if you restrict this ready position to situations were the potential threat is distant, or on an elevated point, it is vastly more efficient than any other ready position. It is generally not a good position for CQB environments.

The high ready involves lowering the butt of the rifle to a point just forward of the firing-side hip at the belt line. The muzzle is positioned so that it appears, visually, just below the line of sight to the target. The line of sight is "eyes – muzzle – target." To bring the rifle from high ready to a firing position, keep the handguard in the support hand in place and pivot the rifle at that point, bringing the butt into the shoulder. When the stock weld and sight picture are established, you are ready to shoot.

Low Ready

The *low ready* position begins with the rifle already mounted into the shoulder. The muzzle is lowered to a position approximately 45 degrees from horizontal, so that the "toe" of the stock is in contact with the shoulder at all times. The lower body is positioned as in a standard firing position. This is the preferred ready position for situations where a specific immediate threat is anticipated, such as in the CQB environment, or when conducting an area search. As in all ready positions, the trigger finger is off the trigger, and the safety lever is generally positioned ON. If facing a specific threat prior to shooting, or assessing the results afterward, don't lower the rifle all the way to 45 degrees, but only low enough to be able to see what you need to see. This usually means lowering the muzzle slightly, just below the line of sight. This is called *contact ready*, and it will allow you to respond to a specific threat or a failure to stop much more quickly than at a full low ready.

Low Inside Ready

The *low inside ready* (also known as *indoor ready*) is a variation of the low ready position. The discussion about the low ready also applies to the low inside ready. The difference comes from an extreme lowering of the muzzle, to the point where the support hand actually touches the support-side leg. The advan-

The low ready position.

The low ready provides a good mix of readiness and visibility in any environment.

The low ready position, as seen here, allows the operator to keep the weapon system an instant away from deployment.

The low inside ready is intended for environments requiring greater visibility and/or weapon control.

tage of this position is it provides the officer with the ability to move quickly from point to point without snagging the muzzle on obstacles. Note that this, like all ready positions, is *preparatory to a firing position*. They are NOT positions of relaxation. Additionally, the officer should employ the tactical sling.

The contact ready is approximately halfway between low ready and "on target."

The patrol ready is a low intensity/low threat level position which is less fatiguing than the other positions. This position probably originated with British forces.

Sometimes a low profile is what is needed. In such cases, the low-profile carry allows the rifle to be retained in a manner that is not visible at a distance (i.e., to TV cameras).

Port Arms Position

The *port arms* position is actually not a "tactical" position, but rather a quick-movement position. There are times when getting somewhere *right now* will be more important than maintaining the ability to shoot immediately. Of greater concern may be protecting the rifle from the environment or bystanders, as well as controlling the muzzle.

Presenting the rifle into a firing position from port arms is slow in comparison to doing so from the other positions, but not so much so that port arms is not an effective carry method for anything other than running from one position to the next. The butt of the rifle is held low at the primary-side waistline, and the muzzle is held high at or about the support-side shoulder.

Patrol Ready Position

Patrol ready was probably invented by British soldiers and has occasionally been called the *UK-ready*. It is similar to the low ready except that the buttstock is tucked under the arm. This is a good position for long-term carry in the field when the threat level is low.

Offhand Firing Position

10

Body and spirit I surrendered whole
To harsh instructors – and received a soul.
> —Rudyard Kipling, "The Wonder," *Epitaphs*, 1919

The offhand position is the least stable of all the firing positions. The advantage of this position comes from its speed of assumption and in cases where the terrain does not allow any other firing position. There are times when the threat will appear *right now,* and you have no time to get into any other position. If there is no immediate urgency to shoot, and if the terrain allows it, you should use a supported position. Remember the rule: *If you can get closer—do so, and if you can get steadier—do so.*

To assume the offhand firing position face approximately 60 degrees to the right of the target line with the legs straight but relaxed. Hold the head erect, and raise the rifle from the ready position until the cheek and the stock come together

The offhand position is the quickest to assume, yet it is also the least steady. In this photo an SF trooper shoots at 100 meters with an FN rifle.

The offhand firing position.

The business end of the offhand firing position. Notice the perpendicular relationship between the primary and support arms.

and the sights are aligned on the target at the level of your shooting eye. The feet, knees, hips, and shoulders are squared off to each other with no twist in the torso.

The support elbow is held directly perpendicular and underneath the rifle. If there is any variance to either side, the shots may tend to string horizontally on the target. The support hand is merely a platform for the rifle to rest on. It "supports" the fore-end but does not "grasp" it.

The firing arm is held roughly at the same level as the shoulder. The firing hand grips the pistol grip as high up as possible, allowing the trigger finger to operate the trigger in the prescribed manner.

Note that the offhand is arrived at from a ready position. As soon as the decision is made to mount the rifle, the safety lever is disengaged, but the trigger finger does not contact the trigger until the rifle arrives in position.

Using the sling like a "hasty sling" for a shooting aid or support is not advised. Not only is a sling not much of an aid to accuracy unless the rifle is fired from a supported position, but using such an aid is not wise with weapons such as the AR-15 rifle because of its dual receiver system. Additionally, many other rifle systems come "as-issued" with tactical slings that are ill-suited for accuracy aids. To be of value, a sling intended as a shooting aid must be *tight*. Deploying such a tight sling with some of these rifles will invariably change its point of impact, causing the shot to go other than where intended. This change may not be much, but it may be enough to miss.

Another point of focus is the practice of placing the support hand under the magazine instead of under the fore-end. This not only takes too much time to do, but it also dramatically reduces the availability of follow-up shots due to diminished recoil recovery. If you have time to assume such a position, you also have the time to get supported. There may be a time when such a support hand position may be indicated, but it falls into the realm of specialized techniques.

After you've fired the necessary shots, you do not relax everything and allow your readiness to go to pieces. Recover to the contact ready position and subsequently to the low ready position to assess the threat. There have been many times when a suspect has been well and solidly hit by an officer, but without being stopped immediately. You must be ready for follow-up shots. After determining that the adversary has been stopped (usually observe for about a second or so), begin scanning to the left, reassess the suspect, and then scan to the right. This is to make sure there are no other suspects in the area that may become threats to the officers, as well as to make certain that there are no officers or citizens entering the line of fire. This is called the after-action assessment, and it must be completed after every firing drill.

In CQB situations, there will be little time to stop and assume a perfect offhand shooting stance as operators move quickly through doors and around obstacles. The stance used in these cases is similar, demonstrates a more aggressive lean, and is less bladed in order to allow aggressive forward movement. The feet, knees, hips, and shoulders are squared to the target area, and the primary side foot leads the support side foot slightly. The elbows are rotated inward slightly, creating some isometric tension in the upper body.

This position facilitates a number of desirable aspects of CQB shooting. It allows controlled two- to three-round bursts (depending on team SOP), it makes for easy shooting on the move, and it allows operators to engage subjects without mitigating the momentum of the team in assault.

In CQB environments, such as when conducting an entry or shooting while moving, the offhand position is identical to the stance used with a submachine gun. This should come as no surprise since the rifle is then being used in SMG territory.

Squatting Firing Position

11

It is not sufficient that the soldier must shoot; he must shoot well.

—Napoleon (1769–1821)

The squatting firing position is the first supported shooting position and also the quickest to assume and quit. The squatting position is useful when cover is too low to use a higher firing position. It is also useful when the ground is covered with debris, preventing a lower or body contact position.

To assume the squatting position, face the target line approximately 30 to 45 degrees with the rifle in a ready position. Disengage the safety and begin to mount the rifle to the shoulder as in the offhand position.

As you do so, lower your body by bending your knees until the rear part of your thighs are resting on your calf muscles. Keep the heels of your feet on the ground and lean forward with your elbows extending well past your knees. The support-side

The squatting position—useful for debris-covered ground or for areas covered in medium-height foliage.

Beginning from a standard ready position . . .

begin to squat, lowering your body until your hamstrings touch your calves.

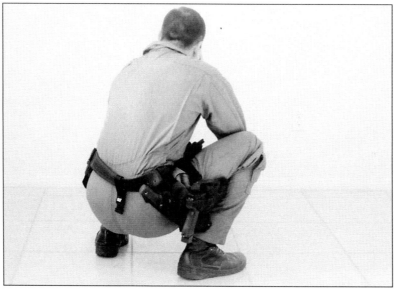

Fine points of the squatting position: feet flat on the deck, elbows inside the knees, solid bone support.

The author demonstrates the fine points of the squatting position to a group of police officers.

triceps will be resting on the flat part of the support-side knee; the primary-side arm will be blocked on the inside of the primary-side knee.

The support hand supports the fore-end but does not grasp it. The stock weld is maintained with the cheek on the stock. After you've fired the necessary shot(s), assess the threat without quitting the position. Only after the threat is over do you stand up and scan left and right.

If you have physical difficulty assuming the squatting position, the alternative is to use the kneeling position.

Kneeling Firing Position

You don't hurt 'em if you don't hit 'em.

—Lt. Gen. Lewis "Chesty" Puller

Kneeling is as useful, tactically speaking, as squatting, and fits the same circumstances. Kneeling is favored by those with physical injuries that prevent the assumption of a squatting position.

To assume a kneeling position, face the target line in a ready position. Step across the target line with the support side foot. If you can imagine that you are standing on a clock face with the target line at 12 o'clock, you would be stepping to 1 o'clock. Pivot the primary-side foot 90 degrees away from the target line so that when you assume the position, the primary-side knee is close to 90 degrees to the line of fire.

As the rifle is mounted into the firing position, sit down on the primary-side foot. Ideally, the foot

Begin from a standard ready position.

Step across the midline with the support-side foot (to approximately 1 o'clock).

Above: Now simply lower the body and sit back until the primary-side buttock rests on the primary-side heel.

Right: Fine points of the kneeling position: buttock on the heel, support triceps on the support-side knee, three points of contact on the deck—toe, knee, and support foot.

would be resting on the ground toes-back. This allows for immediate withdrawal if needed, and it allows you to sit down on the heel. The position may be modified for the individual by resting the foot toes-down or sideways.

Place the support elbow well forward of the knee, with the back of the arm resting on the knee for support. Do not place the elbow point on the point of the knee, as this destroys stability. Hold the primary elbow at shoulder level or slightly below. Shift your weight forward onto the support-side leg.

There are other kneeling firing positions. One is the double kneeling, which allows for more efficient use of cover. This

involves keeping both knees on the deck, providing a lower profile behind cover. The other position is the standard kneeling, but without supporting the elbow on the knee. This is used to direct the fire at upward angles when engaging at close quarters in circumstances where the background is less than ideal.

Sitting
Firing
Position

Good marksmanship is always the most important thing for the infantry.
—Gen. Gerhard von Scharnhorst, 1812

The sitting firing position is useful for circumstances where a static position must be maintained for a long period of time but where greater accuracy than what is offered by kneeling or squatting is required. The sitting position is extremely stable once it is understood. Moreover, sitting allows a greater variance of elevation (in terms of up-angle or down-angle shots) than any other position.

Again, as in the other positions, begin with the rifle in a ready position. Face the target line at 30 to 45 degrees. Step across the primary-side foot with the support-side foot. Using the clock-face analogy, step to 5 o'clock. This places you with the feet crossed.

Now, simply begin to mount the rifle into firing position as you sit down. The timing should be such that as the rifle is mounted your rear end will hit the deck.

Begin from a standard ready position, such as the patrol ready.

Maintaining balance and weapon control, cross the feet, one over the other.

Above: Lower the body until the buttocks hit the deck.

Right: Key points of the sitting position—edges of the feet on the deck; elbows supported on the knees.

You may elect to keep your feet crossed or separate them outward about a shoulder width, depending on your body type. Lean well forward and place the backs of both arms on your knees. If you utilize the cross-legged version, the left leg will be crossed over the right leg so that the outer part of the calf is against the inside part of the foot. You may also keep the legs crossed but extend them outward if the back muscles are tight. If you utilize the open-legged version, place the support-side elbow well forward of the support-side knee, and block the primary-side elbow on the inside of the right knee. Hold the feet out slightly farther than your knees to allow the leg muscles to relax in position.

Again, after the required shot, proceed through the after-action assessment procedure. To recover from sitting, move to a

kneeling position first and then stand up. Do not abandon hand positions on the rifle on the way up, but rather remain able to shoot at every point on the way. Be particularly careful of muzzle control.

Prone
Firing
Position

14

Prone is the most stable of the firing positions, and a good shot can hit about as well from prone as he can from a bench rest. The advantage of prone is precision, but it has several disadvantages as well. The first of these is that it calls for flat ground, since it offers little in terms of elevation adjustment. Second, it requires an accommodating surface. Lying prone on a rocky surface or on a sizzling rooftop does not aid in the accuracy department. Third, the line of sight between target and rifle must be free of intervening cover or obstructions. Fourth, it takes some time to get into and out of.

To assume the prone position, face 30 to 45 degrees off from the target line. You will be dropping along that angular line, but the rifle will be pointed toward the target line.

Drop to both knees, careful to avoid "pole-vaulting" the rifle if you are at the low inside ready. Release the support-hand grip on the fore-end and advance it onto the ground in front of you. You will now be in a half push-up position with the rifle in the primary hand.

Thrust the rifle forward, stopping your fall on the primary-side lat muscle. Now roll toward the support side and resume the two-handed position on the rifle.

If any lateral adjustment of the natural point of aim is needed, rotate the axis of the spine. Be certain that the support elbow is directly under the rifle and not pushed right or left. The rifle is cradled by the support hand and not grasped by it.

The upper body is off the ground, and breathing is not compromised. The legs are spread apart some 30 degrees, with the toes out and heels on the ground. Be certain that no part of the rifle touches the ground.

After firing the requisite shot, conduct the after-action assessment. To quit the prone, release the support hand from the rifle and place it alongside the support-side chest. Push yourself up into a double kneeling position and grip the weapon with both hands. Scan left and right and resume the standing ready position.

There are other prone positions that are suitable for special circumstances in the urban environment. One of them is the roll-over prone. This position involves rolling over onto the primary side with the rifle horizontal to the deck. The firing elbow is rolled under the body, and the fore-end is stabilized with the support hand. This is very similar to the pistol roll-over prone position. Its utility lies in enabling the operator to fire under low obstructions. The sight picture will be a little different, so practicing it is essential before deploying from roll-over prone.

Another on-the-deck position is the supine. Some call it the reverse roll-over prone. In the supine position you are on your back, and the rifle, in position to fire, is across your chest. The shoulder pocket may not be available, since the primary elbow must be kept as flat against the body as possible. Similarly, you must keep your feet as flat on the deck as you can. The fore-end is supported by a reverse grip (from what is standard) with the

Beginning from a low ready . . .

. . . drop to both knees

Allow the support hand to break your forward fall and lower your body down to the deck.

Assume a proper prone firing position. Key points—heels are on the deck, pelvis is on the deck, body is up on the elbows, support arm is as close to perpendicular as possible with the deck, and primary arm is close to perpendicular.

support hand. This position is useful for shooting when using a sidewalk curb for cover.

Both of these additional positions may be worked at the same time as standard prone. It is a simple matter, if range facilities allow, to place three targets in a triangle format. One target will be at 12 o'clock, the others will be at 3 o'clock and 9 o'clock, respectively. On the command, go to standard prone and engage the first target. Transition to roll-over prone and engage the 9 o'clock target. Keeping the muzzle in a safe direction, transition to supine and engage the 3 o'clock target.

SPECIAL NOTE: In all firing positions it is important to remember that the shooter's body is the gun mount. It not only stabilizes the rifle for efficient sighting and firing, but it also affects the placement of those shots. Consequently, your firing position must be as solid and stable as you can make it.

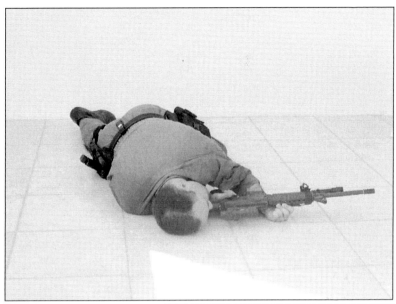

The roll-over prone, a modification from traditional prone, is useful for urban areas with low cover.

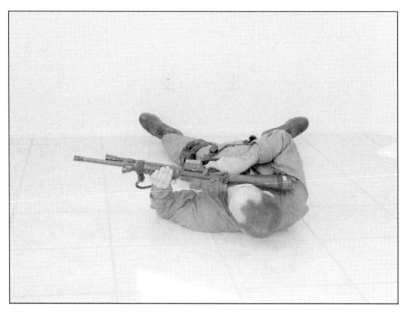

The reverse roll-over prone (actually the supine position) is another specialty position used for firing over a sidewalk curb.

Once the basic positions are learned, you must cultivate the position to fit your body as well as the terrain on which you are deploying. The basic principle of practical marksmanship is to *get as close as you can, but no closer, and to get as steady in position as the situation allows.*

Any system or technique that enhances your ability to hit should be investigated. One of these is the field rest. A field rest is not a position itself; rather, it is the skillful use of the terrain to assist you in maintaining stability. Often, a field rest may also be used, to some degree, as cover or concealment. In all cases, the rifle must not touch the rest itself, but only the hand of the shooter, which is, in turn, rested.

The rest may be a part of your gear, such as a backpack. It may also be an architectural structure such as a fence, post, or vehicle. The use of a field rest enhances accuracy about 30 percent.

Be certain to practice your manipulations, such as reloading and malfunction clearing, from prone as well as from standing positions. If your manipulations do not work well from the prone position, then it's time to change them. What will you do, for example, if you are under fire and you need to clear a stoppage . . . stand up?

Deploying the Rifle from Sling-Arms

15

The sling is to the rifle what the holster is to the pistol.

—Marc Fleischmann

A slingless rifle is a cumbersome dead weight when both hands are needed, or if there is a malfunction requiring a transition to a secondary weapon. Additionally, a good sling secures the rifle to the body, enhancing weapon retention. The bottom line is that all tactical rifles must have a sling system.

There are many different types of slings available today. By far, the most useful is any sort that allows the slung rifle to hang, muzzle down, in front of the chest. The first true tactical sling was probably developed by Heckler & Koch. It is a double loop-type sling that, although somewhat complicated, does a fine job of keeping the rifle in the right place.

Some have improved on the H&K slings by

making the attachment method fit more weapons. Manufacturing materials have also improved. One such sling is the Giles sling, which is virtually identical to the H&K sling, save for its different attachment method and materials.

Another sling type is the Bungee sling. Initially designed for breaching shotguns, the Bungee sling allows the weapon to hang very close to the body. This minimizes dealing with a loose weapon yet still allows ease of deployment, since the Bungee stretches to 250 percent of its normal length.

The final sort of sling is a simple nylon strap (aka "the AR-15 silent sling"). This simple sling attaches via the weapons' sling mounts and works like a conventional sling.

Not only should you be able to drop the rifle to the sling and transition to your handgun if the weapon system malfunctions, but it's also very important that you be able to present from sling. Think about it: if your rifle does not fire when you press the trigger on a close-quarters adversary, do you stand around fiddling with your rifle, trying to make it "go," or do you drop it on the sling, grab your pistol, and neutralize the threat? This simple transition drill teaches one of the most useful skills that a tactical rifleman can develop.

Other times, you may have the rifle along, but you are not expecting an immediate attack. At such times, you often need both hands to communicate, type, set up command post, and so on. If the moment of truth arrives at such a time, you'd better be able to deploy from sling . . . right now.

When dealing with the tactical slings, transitions and presentations are greatly simplified. To transition to the pistol, abandon the firing grip on the rifle and go for the holstered pistol. Simultaneously, move the muzzle down to the support side with the support hand. As the pistol leaves the holster, the support hand abandons the rifle as well. Eventually both hands meet and the problem is solved. The presentation from sling is also simplified because the rifle is almost already in the low ready. Simply position the hands appropriately on the rifle and lift it into firing position.

Things are a little more complex when dealing with stan-

One of the most useful points of the tactical sling is in the event of a stoppage. Simply move the rifle off to the support side while obtaining the backup weapon.

dard sling systems. I experimented with various methods and found them all lacking, but with a little effort they will all suffice, although not as well as a tactical sling. The best methods I've found were developed by two LAPD officers, Officer Dean Gizzi and Detective Marc Fleischmann, for their department's shotgun program. To transition to the pistol with a standard sling-equipped rifle, release the grip of the support hand and regrasp the handguard with a palm-down position. Loop the sling over the head as the primary hand grabs the pistol. As the rifle falls on the sling, muzzle down, both hands meet in a standard firing position. This position of the rifle is called "scramble carry."

An alternate transition from the same officers involves situations where a more secure carry method is needed with less urgent circumstances of transition. Abandon the support hand position and grab the sling, opening up the loop area. The primary hand throws the rifle over the support arm and head, laying the rifle across the back, muzzle down to the support side. This is called "climbing carry."

To transition from scramble carry back into a firing position, grab the fore-end and simply lift the rifle off the neck, being careful about muzzle direction, and into a low ready. To transition from scramble carry into climbing carry, thrust the support arm through the loop. To transition from climbing carry to low ready, use the primary hand to lift the sling up and over the head so that the rifle is now carried over the support-side shoulder, muzzle down. Now the support hand grasps the fore-end and lifts it up into a low ready position as the primary hand finds the pistol-grip area of the rifle.

Some slings may be used to enhance the accuracy of some rifles. I do not believe that this is a useful technique for tactical rifles. The only slings that actually provide any sort of support are the military type or the scout type. Neither of these slings is useful in CQB environments. Moreover, using such a sling may provide a different point of aim than what is seen without the sling. The hasty sling, or the standard sling looped around the support-side arm, does nothing at all. Better to spend the time

For weapons not equipped with tactical slings, but rather with conventional two-point slings, the technique designed by Officer Dean Gizzi is very useful.

Thrust the support hand, like a spear, through the opening between rifle and sling.

Now roll the rifle over the head and allow it to drop on its sling behind your back in a climbing carry format.

As soon as you relinquish control of the rifle, get the backup weapon system into the fight.

One method to recover the rifle from this position is to simply roll the head under the sling and recover back into a ready position.

Another solution to the two-point sling transition is the Fleischmann Transition. This involves rotating the support hand to a reverse grip on the fore-end.

Take the rifle, muzzle down, and loop it over the neck, maintaining muzzle control.

This allows the backup weapon to be deployed quickly.

For low-profile or weapon-control requirements, simply reach around the back with the primary hand and grasp the receiver. Pull the weapon behind the back, concealing from view.

perfecting the position, and other fundamentals, instead of trying to make the sling an accuracy aid.

Slings are of paramount importance to the rifle when used in urban close-quarters environments. Get the best one you can, and don't leave home without it.

Reloading the Rifle

16

One who has few must prepare against the enemy; one who has many makes the enemy prepare against him.

—Sun Tzu, *The Art of War*

If the officer does his part, he will rarely *need* to reload in a tactical situation. But neglecting to practice doing so is like saying that you will probably never have a flat tire so a spare in the trunk is not necessary.

There are three circumstances where reloading is important. The first circumstance involves reloading to full capacity once the initial confrontation appears to be over. Urban gunfights are characterized by sudden high-intensity, short duration violence, after which the bad guys (unless they have been stopped by the officers) either take cover and hide, or flee. The fight may not necessarily be over, but it appears to be. Before the officer commits to leave his position or execute any other action, he should reload his partially depleted rifle to full capacity . . . just in case. This is called the tactical reload. It is executed during a perceived pause in the fight, when there is no urgent need to keep shooting, and where the officer desires to save the partially depleted magazine.

TACTICAL RELOAD PROCEDURE

The tactical reload may be performed from any position. From the low ready, bring the rifle butt under the primary arm, high in the armpit.

Maintaining focus on the threat, remove the depleted magazine in the rifle and secure it in a pocket, or even down the front of your shirt with the support hand. Also with the support hand, obtain a fresh magazine and insert it into the rifle's magazine well. It is important to push it up and hear it "click" as it seats into place. Tug on it slightly to insure that it is seated. Now strike the bolt catch with the support hand. This is done just in case the rifle is out of battery (shot empty) and will allow the bolt to move into battery and chamber a round.

The first notice you will have in a fight that you've run out of ammo will be that your weapon system won't fire.

Other than a quick transition to the pistol, to fix the problem you will have to identify the problem (in this case, bolt locked open, empty gun!).

Step one is to locate a replacement magazine. Notice that the weapon system is kept on target.

Step two is to eject the empty "on board" magazine and simultaneously bring the replacement magazine toward the weapon

Insert the magazine. Seat it until you feel it and hear it "click" into place. Now tug on it to make sure it is seated.

Using the support-hand palm, hit the bolt catch, thereby releasing the bolt and chambering a round.

Back in the fight.

The proper grasp of a magazine for reloading during a gunfight. Notice the little finger curled underneath to prevent losing control of the magazine in inclement weather.

If you believe that your magazine's capacity has been depleted by about half, then a tactical reload is in order. Begin by removing the depleted magazine.

Secure the depleted magazine in the waistband, tactical vest pocket, or down the front of your shirt.

Obtain a replacement magazine with the support hand. Notice that the rifle is maintained on the threat area. Do not lower the weapon system; keep it ready to fight.

Insert the fresh magazine, seat it until you feel and hear it "click," and tug on it to make sure it is seated

Back in the fight.

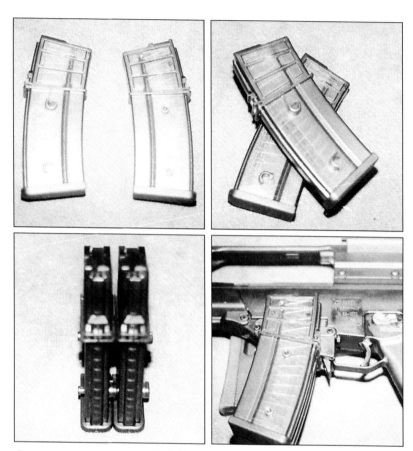

Some weapons, such as the HK G36, feature magazines that attach to one another, thereby facilitating the reloading process.

Resume the two-handed hold on the rifle and mount into the low ready position.

If you have large hands and can handle having both magazines in the one hand (this is easier done with 20-round magazines), you can obtain the fresh magazine first and then move to the magazine well. Holding both magazines in the same hand, extract the old, and insert the new. This is much faster if you can make it work for you, but it is not advisable if you have small mitts! To be sure, I prefer securing the depleted magazine first

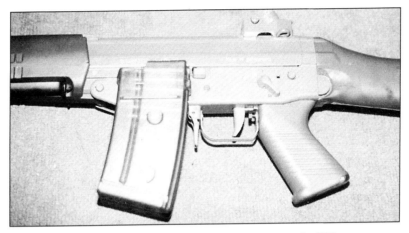

The SIG series of rifles have similar magazine systems to the HK.

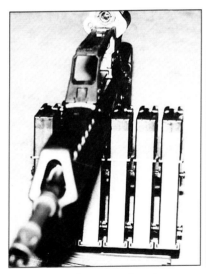

This, like all things, can be taken to extremes. Here a G36 is equipped with six magazines side by side—that adds up to 180 rounds and a very heavy rifle!

The older HK 91/93 and 53 series rifles must have the charging handle and bolt locked open during the reloading sequence.

and then obtaining its replacement. It is too easy to drop one or more magazines when trying to balance them in the hand.

The next situation requiring a reload is similar in nature to the tactical reload but involves a rapidly moving and developing situation. Here you may have fired and solved your immediate tactical problem, but you may be required to rush to the aid of other officers still embattled by armed suspects. In this case, getting to the location of the officers in need precludes the desire to save a partially depleted magazine. This is called an in-battery speedload.

IN-BATTERY SPEEDLOAD PROCEDURE

Keep the rifle in a low ready or firing position. Using the support hand, obtain a fresh magazine. Simultaneously press the magazine release button with the primary hand. This will eject the on-board magazine. Quickly reload the fresh magazine and seat it into the rifle. Always tug on the magazine to insure that it is seated and hit the bolt catch with the palm heel of the support hand. This technique is often done on the move.

The final situation calling for a reload is when you are facing an immediate threat in the open and you press the trigger and nothing happens! This may be one of various occurrences with the rifle. It may be a malfunction, or it may simply be an empty rifle. There are two solutions to this.

TRANSITION TO PISTOL

If the threat is within realistic handgun range, such as in a close-quarters confrontation inside a building, you may elect to transition to your service pistol and engage the threat. When the adversary is so close, the reality is that producing the pistol and shooting is much quicker than any gun manipulation due to the inherent and unavoidable lag time experienced from realization of the problem and implementation of the solution. If the shot does not go off from the rifle, go to the pistol. It's as simple as that! If the threat is outside of realistic handgun distances, you'll have to fix your rifle.

To transition to the pistol, use the tactical sling by releasing the primary hand's grip on the rifle and obtaining a firing grip on the pistol. Simultaneously, bring the support hand (and the rifle) to the support-side hip. Then release your support hand's grip on the rifle and secure a two-handed grip on the pistol, allowing the rifle to hang by the sling in front of your body.

OUT-OF-BATTERY SPEED RELOAD

To solve the problem outside of handgun distances, the first thing you must do is determine the nature of the problem with your rifle.

From the firing position, turn the weapon counterclockwise 45 degrees and look at the ejection port. If the rifle is empty, the bolt will be locked open. Quickly release the support hand and obtain a fresh magazine. Find the magazine release button with the primary hand and press it, releasing the empty magazine. With the support hand, bring the replacement magazine into the magazine well, seating and tugging. Reach up with the support hand palm heel and hit the bolt catch, releasing the bolt and chambering a round.

For training purposes, you will note that we do not automatically fire after changing magazines, or even after clearing malfunctions. This is because you do not want to be conditioned to shoot reflexively after a gun handling operation. Any shots fired must be the result of a conscious controlled decision, not an uncontrolled conditioned reflex.

Malfunction Clearing Procedures

17

The sharp general takes into account not only probable dangers, but also those which may be totally unexpected.
— The Emperor Maurice, *The Strategikon* (c. A.D. 600)

Every manmade tool has the potential to malfunction. In terms of tactical firearms used for defensive purposes, the likelihood of the malfunction occurring at a critical time is great. Knowing how to quickly "fix the problem" and get back into action is of paramount importance. The same rule goes for the malfunction issues as for reloading. If the threat is imminent, go to the pistol.

First, you must understand that a malfunction is a stoppage of the rifle's firing cycle that may be cleared quickly in the field. A so-called jam is a broken part that must be seen to by an armorer and cannot be easily cleared in the field.

Additionally, while an instructor may introduce "dummy" rounds into a magazine to simulate one type of malfunction, there are two others that cannot be induced artificially. The best methods for training the clearance procedures is during dry practice at the range. Here the student places his rifle in the condition resembling the malfunction and is taught how to clear it. Again, there is no "automatic" shooting at the conclusion of the maneuvers.

The rule with malfunction clearing is that *if there is an immediate need to shoot, and the adversary is within realistic handgun distances, a transition to the handgun (as described in the previous chapter) is indicated.* If the threat is outside of realistic handgun distances, then moving to cover is the first consideration. Next, the type of malfunction must be defined, and finally, it must be cleared. The malfunction clearance procedures are useful for all weapon systems, although the operator may be required to modify them slightly to fit his own requirements. There are three types of malfunctions: failure to fire, failure to eject, and feedway stoppage.

FAILURE TO FIRE CLEARANCE PROCEDURE

Set this up by clearing the chamber of any rounds and closing the bolt. Then insert a full magazine into the rifle.

From a firing position, press the trigger and notice the "click" sound. That is the indicator of what you have, and there is no need to analyze the problem any further. Release the support hand from the fore-end and tap and tug the bottom of the magazine to insure that it is fully seated. Simultaneously turn (flip) the rifle 90 degrees clockwise with the ejection port facing down, and rack the charging handle to the rear with the support hand. The key words to remember are:

- Tap
- Tug
- Rack
- Flip

The failure to fire may be caused by an improperly seated magazine, defective magazine, or defective ammunition.

The loudest sound in the world: a "click" when you expected a "bang." The immediate action drill for this involves first hitting the bottom of the magazine.

With the support hand, activate the charging handle (thereby cycling the bolt and ejecting any unfired rounds) while flipping the rifle to the right.

This same clearing drill solves a failure to fire as well as a failure to eject. It is simplicity at its best.

FAILURE TO EJECT CLEARANCE PROCEDURE

Set this one up by pressing the trigger on an empty chamber. Then retract the bolt only far enough to insert an empty cartridge case partially into the ejection port. Then insert a full magazine into the magazine well.

Mount the rifle and press the trigger. This will feel different from the first malfunction. Turn the rifle 45 degrees counterclockwise and inspect the chamber. You will see a partially ejected empty brass cartridge case. That is your clue. The solution is identical to the first one:

- Tap
- Tug
- Rack
- Flip

One maneuver solves two problems, keeping with the spirit of simplicity. Failures to eject are often caused by defective springs in the rifle or worn parts in the receiver, in addition to problems with the magazines or ammunition.

FEEDWAY STOPPAGE CLEARING PROCEDURE

This is the most complicated of all malfunctions to clear. To set it up, lock the bolt to the rear. Insert an empty cartridge case into the chamber. Insert a loaded magazine into the rifle and ease the bolt forward by using the charging handle. This creates a condition where two rounds are competing for the chamber at the same time.

Bring the rifle into firing position and press the trigger. Again, you will experience an unusual situation with the trigger. Turn the still-mounted rifle 45 degrees counterclockwise and look into the chamber area. Realizing you have a feedway stoppage, you must first lock the bolt to the rear. Next, strip the onboard magazine out and let it fall. Clear any rounds or cases stuck in the ejection port area by inserting the support hand fingers. Hit the bolt catch, releasing the bolt in the event there is a

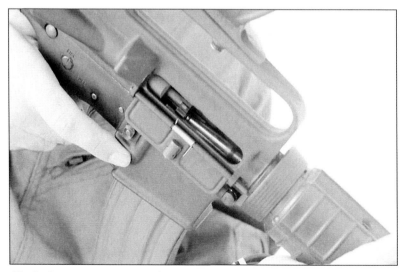

The feedway stoppage occurs when two rounds are competing for the chamber. Sometimes the round begins to feed, but the bolt somehow moves underneath it, trapping it between the top of the bolt and the inside surface of the receiver.

Step one is to identify the problem. It is a wise idea to get behind cover if you're not already there. This one will take a while to fix.

Lock the bolt to the rear.

Strip and discard the "on board" magazine.

Insert the support hand fingers into the magazine well to clear any rounds or cases still stuck in the inside of the receiver.

Strike the bolt catch with the support hand to close the action.

Rack the action three times briskly.

Obtain a fresh magazine, insert it into the magazine well, seat it until you hear and feel a "click," and finally, tug on it to make sure.

Rack the action one final time to chamber a round and get back in the fight.

round in the chamber. Rack the action three or four times to clear out any remaining cartridges. Insert a new magazine into the rifle, and rack the action one final time to chamber a round. The process is summed up as follows:

- Look
- Lock
- Strip
- Clear
- Hit
- Rack
- Insert
- Rack

Tactical Considerations

18

Fortuitous outcomes reinforce poor tactics.

— Sgt. Gary Rovarino, LASD/SEB (Ret.)

This chapter contains a number of tactical tips and guidelines intended to enhance operational capabilities. In addition to these tips is a discussion of tactical terminology used in SWAT. The likelihood of rifle team members setting up a containment on a suspect stronghold while other department assets (SWAT, negotiators, etc.) are brought into play is great, and it is useful if we all speak the same language. Additionally, riflemen may be placed in a situation where they will operate alone, and they should be well versed in tactical issues. Keep the following principles in mind during all tactical operations.

TACTICAL GUIDELINES

1) *Use your senses to look for target indicator (TIs).* Primarily, you will rely on your sense of sight (eyes) and your sense of hearing (ears). Do not, however, dismiss the other senses. Your sense of smell as well as touch will provide you with essential data about the whereabouts of the enemy during your search.

Target indicators are anything that will indicate the presence of an adversary. They are often categorized as shine, movement, sound, smell, shape, contrast, human sign, and tactical sign. Some indicators may be very obvious, like the sound of a careful footfall on a creaky wooden floor, the reflection of a hidden adversary on a light fixture, a shadow on the floor in front of you, a flicker of movement in the darkness, or even a gun muzzle protruding from around a corner. TIs may be subtle, such as the sound of fabric scraping against a wall, careful breathing in a darkened room, or an open gate that was previously closed.

Target indicators may also be olfactory. For example, the smell of a smoker in a nonsmoking residence is difficult to miss. Weapons solvents, cologne, body odor, and the more primal human scents may also alert you to the presence of a hostile. Human sign and tactical sign are indicators left behind by sloppy adversaries. Fresh footprints on a dew-covered lawn, cigarette smoke wafting in the air, and palm prints on a foggy glass window are good examples of human sign. Tactical sign consists of any indication that the adversary has modified his environment by his presence. Open windows on a cool day, furniture stacked against a door, and booby traps are all examples of tactical sign. There are others.

You may even feel the adversary's body heat as you search a close-quarters environment such as a small hiding place. I remember experiencing this firsthand during an interior search for a narcotics suspect. He'd fled our initial entry and had run to the rear of the house. After a meticulously slow and thorough search, we reached the only room remaining—the bathroom. He'd been hiding in the cabinet under the sink for over an hour, and I distinctly remember feeling his body heat emanating through the cracks in the door of the cabinet as I moved to open it. Too bad for him!

These subtle, and not-so-subtle, clues will be easily noticed if you are paying attention to your environment. They denote attempts at concealment by those you are searching for. They are hostile and dangerous indications that someone is there, hiding . . . perhaps waiting for you!

2) *Avoid producing target indicators.* Just as you seek target indicators during your search, you must strive not to produce them yourself. Searching either an interior or exterior area for a hostile is 50 percent hunting and 50 percent avoiding being hunted. At such times, stealth is king! Unless you are forced to rush into a confrontation (an active shooter in a crowded shopping mall, for example), take it slow, careful, and methodical. Be quiet, be careful, move slowly, and handle each tactical obstacle individually. If you make a noise unintentionally, stop, look, and listen for any reaction by the adversary for about 60 seconds before proceeding.

3) *Do not assume something is secure until you've checked it out yourself.* Do not rationalize something that is out of place; check it out and be sure. I was once searching a residential area for a psycho who'd tried to hack a couple of citizens with an axe. I was moving along the front of a residence with my back-up man when we heard a faint metallic sound coming from the driveway area. We alerted to the sound (audible target indicator) and began moving down the driveway. Halfway to the backyard that lay beyond it, we heard a clothes dryer operating inside the house. It really sounded like someone had forgotten to empty the change out of their pockets before washing their clothes. We both rationalized that the sound was the metallic sound we'd heard and dismissed the possibility of the villain's presence. After a superficial scan of the yard, we retraced our steps back to the street. As we reached the next driveway, our boy ran out into the street, away from us, ax in hand, from the

When approaching a door, do not let the muzzle fall below the support hand because it will be difficult to raise it back into a firing position quickly. Operate the door and let it open. As soon as you can, get both hands back on the rifle.

yard that we'd just "cleared"! Doom on us! Luckily, everything turned out fine, but don't you make the same mistake! Remember, be dead sure, or be dead!

4) *Within reason, maximize your distance from potential threats and minimize your exposure to them.* This can be taken to extremes, of course, since you can maximize your distance by being back at the station when criminals are shooting up the town. By picking up the rifle you are in effect saying, "I will go in harm's way," and you must close with the adversary. So maximize the distance as much as the tactical situation allows, while still being close enough to affect the outcome. Stay away from corners and any other area that you cannot see beyond as far as the geography will allow. Do not let your muzzle (or feet) protrude into the unsecured space in front of you. Doing so will not only betray your position and intentions, but it may get your weapon snatched away from you. It may even get you killed.

5) *Move tactically.* Keep your balance as you move from one problem to another. Keep your weapon in a low ready or contact ready, poised to fire instantly at any threat. The purpose of any tactical maneuver is to allow your muzzle to cover the potential danger areas as you encounter them. Observe the "three eye principle." This means that your weapon must be oriented at whatever your eyes are looking at. Wherever your eyes go, your weapon must also go. Keep the weapon in a ready position or "hunting" attitude so that it does not obstruct your vision while you search. When moving in open areas, do so briskly, and go around them, not directly through them. Do not run unless you are already under fire. Move at a brisk walk unless approaching a specific danger area. When closing in on a potential danger area, move by using the shuffle step, since it allows greater balance and control.

6) *When it is time to shoot, pay attention to the basics.* My associates and I jokingly call these the "four secrets." They are no secret at all. They are sight alignment, sight picture, trigger

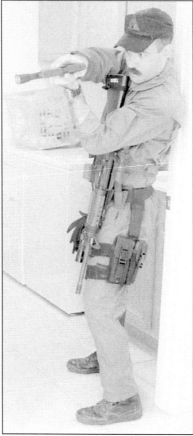

When conducting an angular search, roll out with the rifle just enough to be able to see and shoot.

Don't be afraid to secure the rifle and clear a tight spot with the more compact pistol if you must.

control, and follow-through. These "secrets" will allow you to get fast, solid hits on your adversary in the least amount of time possible in order to keep him from doing the same to you. Remember, you cannot miss fast enough to make a difference! You cannot miss fast enough to win a gunfight! If you cannot hit on demand, all the tactics in the world will be of no use to you.

In close-quarters environments, keep your eyes and rifle muzzle oriented on the potential threat.

Be sure that you look up, as many scenarios will exhibit second-level threats. When clearing a stairway, for example, clear one section at a time.

SPECIFIC OUTDOOR TACTICS

Another tip: when scanning an area for a suspect from a vantage point, it is more efficient visually to scan along a varying vertical axis. This is called an overlapping strip search. This will allow you to examine the same spot several times from varying angles. Such a visual search will enhance the possibility of seeing something you'd missed during previous passes. This means you look out and back instead of back and forth. Change the angle and continue until you've checked the area in question fully.

Use whatever cover is available. Here is one practical application of the roll-over prone for the top of a stairway.

The same situation used as a makeshift rest for the rifleman's support hand.

As long as the length is kept within reason, a shorter rifle is more useful in close quarters than a longer weapon. Top to bottom: Colt Commando, Bushmaster Carbine with ACOG scope, UZI America's Micro Galil.

Avoid silhouetting yourself against the sky or a light background. Remember, if you can be seen, you can be shot. Stay in the shadows if possible. If there is an overhead light where you must deploy, see about turning it off or just break the damn thing. Be careful also about reflective surfaces such as windows. They may give away your position.

When moving in pairs or as a team to a position of containment against an armed suspect, you may use methods borrowed from military tactics. These methods are called traveling overwatch and bounding overwatch and involve mutual support from one team member in a covered position for a second team member that is on the move toward him. These methods may be used to advance as well as to withdraw, such as when rescuing a downed officer or citizen.

When deploying around a building, we normally announce that we will take, for example, the north side, or the southwest corner, and so forth. Sometimes this is confusing, particularly for structures that do not conform to north–south/east–west lines.

The method employed by virtually all SWAT teams is to number the four sides of a structure. The side facing the street (usually the side with the front door) is labeled the Number One side. The count is then followed clockwise, so that the side to the left of the Number One side is called the Number Two side, and so on. If you are deploying to a point that covers two sides, you would say, "I am at the One-Two corner." Once this is understood, it fits all circumstances.

It is also important that the team knows the procedure for counting floors when looking at a tall, multiple-story building. Some teams count the floors from the top down. This is because the architecture on modern buildings often exposes two floors at ground level or conceals them completely. An officer need only say, "Number One side, from the top, floor number two, third window," and everyone will know the spot he is talking about. The method used is not crucial, but everyone must use the same one.

Another very important issue is understanding the difference between cover and concealment. *Cover is anything solid that offers ballistic protection.* That means that you may hide behind it and be reasonably certain that you will not be struck by incoming fire. *Concealment, on the other hand, is anything that hides your presence.* An example of cover would be a solid brick wall. An example of concealment is darkness. Sometimes cover will also offer concealment.

You must always be aware of the environment around which you deploy and be able to discern quality points of cover. Realize also that hard cover will also tend to cause projectiles to ricochet. Projectiles tend to ricochet along a parallel axis to the cover they've struck and at an angle slightly away from it. If you are positioned too close to the point of cover, they might very well ricochet directly into you. The safe distance seems to be approximately six feet back from cover. At six feet, the angle of departure of the ricochet has generally grown to the point where the projectiles will probably bypass you completely.

There are times, however, when you may wish to crowd the point of cover. This is the case when your adversary has a position above yours. In such cases, if you are too distant from your cover, he will be able to bypass your cover and shoot down into your position.

When engaging from behind cover, shoot around and not over it. Resist the temptation to change hands on the weapon. Few people are as accurate with their support side as they are with the primary side. The entire reason to roll out from cover is to hit the threat and stop it.

Realize that cover and other obstacles are a double-edged sword. You may use them to your benefit, but you may also be required to penetrate through your adversary's cover. As a general rule, an officer should not fire blindly into cover hoping to hit the threat. There may be times when only a small portion of the suspect is visible from around his cover and it is preferable to hit that than it is to attempt penetration of the cover without knowing for certain what is behind it. If the cover is light and you know the exact location of the threat, penetrating the cover with fire may be a tactical option to pursue. It is therefore important to know the penetrating capabilities of your rifle system and ammunition.

The most commonly encountered object that an officer must shoot through is glass. Glass is easy to shatter, but it is very hard and tends to damage most bullets. There are different types of glass that present varying degrees of difficulty in penetration. The glass in the side and rear windows of automobiles, for example, is designed to crumble on impact and is very easy to penetrate. The tempered, plastic laminated windshield glass, however, may be a different story. Residential windows are made of relatively light glass and again pose little challenge. Storefront windows, or the glass doors of a business, however, are very difficult to penetrate with .223 ammunition.

Bullets fired through thick glass may shatter the glass, yet not retain enough mass to inflict any wound at all on a threat. Moreover, bullets in the process of getting through the glass may be deflected, along with glass spalling, at varying angles from the point of aim.

The rule about glass is that if you can avoid shooting through it, you would be well advised to do so. If the threat is very close to the glass, the glass does not seem to be very thick, and the shot may be made perpendicular to the target, you may consider taking it. Otherwise, seek alternatives.

There are other items commonly used as cover that may need to be penetrated, such as vehicle bodies and wooden obstacles. Vehicle sheet metal is nearly as difficult to penetrate as glass unless a direct 90-degree shot is taken. Wooden obstacles such as fences or walls are not a problem as long as the shot is taken as close to 90 degrees as possible. Shallow angle shots, on any type of cover, will tend to ricochet or break up and not penetrate.

The foregoing discussion about keeping your distance from cover is not intended to dissuade the use of field supports to aid shooting (aka "barricade shooting"). You may be able to do this as well as keep a safe distance from cover. It is a simple matter to move back from the item intended as cover and use a different item as a field support. The incoming rounds will be encountering your cover, which may be as far as several yards away, while you utilize the closer field support to shoot from. This brings us to the discussion of field-expedient rests.

One of the aspects of placing the shot exactly where it is required is a stable position. Physically, it is very difficult to hold a rifle perfectly still. Even very experienced shooters will have a certain degree of movement in the their most stable positions. To get hits at distance, in addition to the other fundamentals, you must have a stable shooting platform or position.

One of the things that you can do to help enhance the stability of your rifles (and yourself) is to shoot from a rested or supported position. Many sniper operators, for example, have Harris Bipods attached to their rifles. This is a very worthwhile addition to a precision rifle, but it should not become a crutch. It does not belong on a tactical rifle.

Even for snipers, there are times when a Harris Bipod will not be of use because of the tactical requirements of the situation at hand. Perhaps you will be required to shoot from a standing position, such as to take a shot over the top of a fence. Perhaps you've deployed inside a residence and are planning to shoot from a seated position through the window. Or perhaps you are called to make the shot hastily, due to a dynamically evolving situation. Knowing how to quickly use a rest—any rest—will help you to place that round where it needs to go . . . with extreme precision.

One word of warning: whatever rest or support is used, *do not rest the rifle on a hard surface.* You can rest the rifle on a soft surface, which in turn is rested on a hard surface, but not hard to hard. Doing so will interfere with barrel harmonics and cause your shot to go errant.

Perhaps the most easily available support is a rucksack. Most riflemen carry their gear in some sort of ruck, and it is a simple matter to unshoulder the pack, let it hit the deck, and fall down on it with the rifle.

Furniture may be configured into a hasty shooting platform. I've used this technique, and it is both comfortable and stable. It involves placing two chairs back to back. You sit in one (backwards) and use the back of the other one as a rifle rest. Be sure to insert a jacket or some other soft, recoil absorbing material between the rifle and the rest.

If a standing or kneeling shot is called for, you can use a technique called the "tree rest." This is borrowed from African big game hunters, who take long shots on plains. They developed a method of using a tree to support the rifle. I first read about this method in one of Peter Capstick's books and practiced it firsthand at Jeff Cooper's old rifle course.

In urban operations, you can use any vertical surface. A telephone pole, traffic light, or even the side of a building can replace the "tree." To use this method, place the flat of your support hand against the surface, so that the thumb and index finger are free. Now place the rifle in the crook of the hand, using the index finger to cushion the rifle from the hard surface.

Among sniper operators, sandbags are very popular for use in range and tactical environments because they allow great stability. A tactical rifleman may not carry a sandbag around, but he can improvise. A dog food bag makes a great sandbag, as do sacks of grain in rural areas. Even a bag of barbecue briquettes may be used in a pinch.

Finally, if no rest is available for your rifle, you may still find a rest for yourself. In any position other than prone, you may be able to lean your back against something solid, such as a house or wall, to stabilize your shooting. This will minimize the inherent movement in each shooter's position.

It is important to be tactically flexible. Part of that includes using the immediate environment and knowing about the natural and field expedient rests available.

Low-Light Operations

19

Darkness is the friend of the skilled infantryman.
— Capt. Sir Basil Liddell Hart, *Thoughts on War*, 1944

Excluding planned tactical operations, a good amount of our job as riflemen dictates reacting to what criminals have done. Most crimes of violence tend to occur during hours of darkness (2000 hrs. to 0400 hours). Most officer-involved shootings (70 percent) occur, again, during hours of darkness. The likelihood of being required to deploy against an armed adversary in reduced light is great.

Operating in reduced light has advantages as well as disadvantages. The darkness belongs to whoever wants to take advantage of it. Darkness can hide the rifleman and cover his movements. It facilitates deception and promotes confusion in the suspect. But there is another side to the coin.

It is extremely difficult to shoot well, at distance, in darkness. Shooting in darkness presents two very distinct problems. One is the necessity to positively identify the suspect. Seeing a "shadow" is not enough; you must be certain. The second problem is visibility of the sights or scope reticle. Following are some things that a rifleman might do in order to mitigate the effects of darkness:

- The first thing is to get out and shoot in the darkness. Night shooting with a rifle is vastly different from day-time shooting. An easy shot at high noon, for example, may be nearly impossible at midnight on a moonless night. In short, if you know your limits, you can plan around them.
- If your rifle is equipped with an optical sight, find what the best setting is for night shooting. Our pupils dilate to about 7mm in total darkness. The scope is most effective when it produces a cone of light of similar diameter. A 40mm objective lens scope, for example, is best set at 6X for low-light shooting. Other scopes designed for tactical rifles have larger-than-usual exit pupils to allow more light into the optical system.
- Some scopes have low-light capability built in. The Trijicon ACOG, for example has a tritium illuminated reticle which is quite easy to see in darkness. In training, we've been able to get center body hits on moonless nights out to 50 yards. There are other optics available with similar properties. Some optics are even designed to incorporate detachable NVDs. Although I have not had the opportunity to work with these personally, I've heard very good reports from operators who use them.
- At night, in order to see better and guarantee the shot, you may be required to stalk closer to the suspect in order to have a clear shot. We must be able to guarantee our shots, and if the original firing position does not allow enough visibility or is too distant to guarantee the shot, we must move closer.
- Use your creativity. You might be able to pre-position remote lighting. For example, you may be able to place

a patrol car, with headlights on high beam, down the street. This may provide enough ambient light to see the suspect . . . and the reticle.

- Use ambient light to your advantage. In one deployment I recall, the suspect graciously left his porch light on, which allowed us great visibility as he exited the house.

It is also possible to use a Sure-Fire flashlight to complement the rifle in close-range encounters (within 25 yards). These may be attached semipermanently, or you may use a standard patrol Sure-Fire. With the later circumstance, you turn the base tailcap until the light comes on. Then back it off until the light just goes off. You will notice that any lateral pressure on the tailcap will turn the light on.

Simply lay the light alongside the rifle's fore-end and assume the usual firing position. When you need to illuminate something, just squeeze the light. This works well out to 50 yards or so. That should tell you something about the deployment distances that insure success at night.

The Sure-Fire flashlight products are about the best available. In my opinion, all tactical weapons that are likely to see deployment in low light should have a dedicated light mount. That goes for patrol as well as SWAT.

A technique taught at the FBI Countersniper School involves deploying a team of two officers to engage a threat in a darkened environment. The officers employ a countdown system. One officer is in position, ready to shoot. The other officer is positioned next to the designated shooter with a powerful flashlight. The count begins at "three." On "two," flashlight man lights up the threat. On "one," the officer shoots. The light is turned off immediately, and the team changes positions.

The observer, if any, has the same duties in reduced light as he does at high noon. Having an (NVD) is almost mandatory. Not only must the rifle team be able to move into position in the dark, but it must be able to see everything in the area of responsibility once it arrives.

Another consideration is that in the confusion of night,

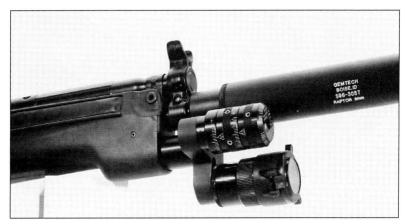

There are a number of equipment options for night operators. From IR-visible lasers to white light attachments, the tactical rifle can be equipped as needed. (Photo courtesy of Laser Products.)

The AR-15/M16 rifle can be equipped with visible or IR-visible laser modules for operators using night vision goggles (NVGs), as well as with the obligatory white light systems. (Photo courtesy of Laser Products.)

The newer Sure-Fire models M500A and M500B are the brightest white lights available. These lights are actually painful to look at and are just the ticket for close-quarters fighting.

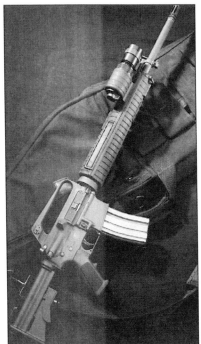

The Laser Products Forend is available for short and standard handguards. (Photo Courtesy of Laser Products.)

The quintessential CQB carbine—an M-4 with Vortex Flash Suppressor, ACOG Sight System, and Laser Products White Light System.

entry team members may be indistinguishable from the background . . . or the suspect. If the observer (or rifleman) is equipped with an NVD, the entry team may be identified with Infra-Red Chemlights attached to their assault gear. These will be visible only to the NVD-equipped observer or rifleman.

Supplemental infrared (IR) lighting, invisible to the non-NVD-equipped suspect, may be employed to see with more detail into the target area. The observer may also be able to direct the rifleman to a particular point with his use of the NVD. A great deal can be seen through a daytime scope if you know what you are looking at. The observer with the NVD can tell you what to look at.

NVDs do have disadvantages, however. They are monochromatic, which means that colors are not distinguishable. Night vision, unless equipped with an IR light source, requires ambient light to use. They tend to confuse distances due to lack of depth perception cues present in lighted environments. Finally, using an NVD washes out the dark adaptation of the

If resources do not allow a dedicated light system, a standard light can be substituted with some creativity.

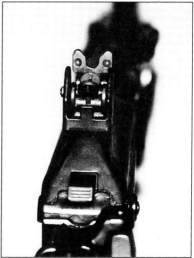

Tritium-equipped "night sights" are available for many weapons and may be an option to examine if your encounters are likely to occur in low light. The Galil low-light sights are some of the best available on any rifle. (Photo Courtesy of Cory Trapp, SAS Products.)

A short-barreled rifle requires flash suppression, not muzzle brakes.

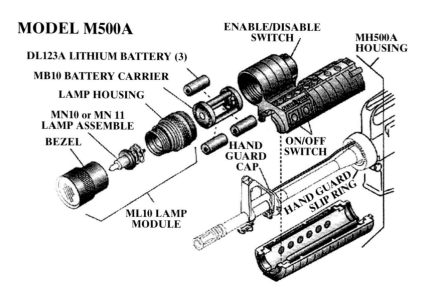

MODEL M500A

ENABLE/DISABLE SWITCH

MH500A HOUSING

DL123A LITHIUM BATTERY (3)

MB10 BATTERY CARRIER

LAMP HOUSING

MN10 or MN 11 LAMP ASSEMBLE

BEZEL

HAND GUARD CAP

ON/OFF SWITCH

HAND GUARD/ SLIP RING

ML10 LAMP MODULE

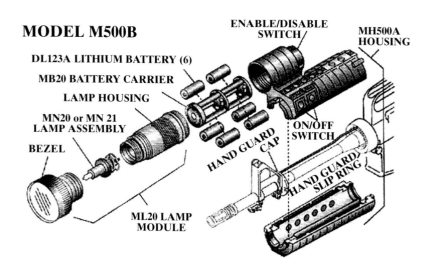

MODEL M500B

ENABLE/DISABLE SWITCH

MH500A HOUSING

DL123A LITHIUM BATTERY (6)

MB20 BATTERY CARRIER

LAMP HOUSING

MN20 or MN 21 LAMP ASSEMBLY

BEZEL

HAND GUARD CAP

ON/OFF SWITCH

HAND GUARD/ SLIP RING

ML20 LAMP MODULE

The Laser Products M500A and M500B light systems. Exploded views.

eyes. This will take from 30 minutes to 2 hours to restore. If no NVD is available, the rifle team must use as much ambient light as possible to scout the location.

Ideally, the rifle team should have a night rifle, as well as a day rifle. If such sophistication is prohibitively expensive, a simple NVD monocular in the rifleman's kit is a good and relatively inexpensive substitute.

Operating and, if necessary, shooting in dark environments is a very necessary part of the rifleman's job. With a few items of equipment, and some training effort, you can be well prepared to handle such eventualities, and . . . own the night.

Shooting on the Move and Close-Contact Techniques

20

Force does not exist for mobility, but mobility for force.
—Rear Admiral Alfred Thayer Mahan,
"Lessons of the War with Spain"

The ability to shoot as you move from one point or obstacle to the next is very important. The entire reason and purpose for any tactical maneuver, whether slow or quick, is to allow you to cover the next potential danger area with your muzzle. Sometimes you must also shoot on the move as you advance toward another position. You may even wish to aggressively close on an adversary to shoot him on the advance in order to put him on the defensive or to enable yourself to execute a more precise shot.

Some theorists have suggested that you can simply stand fast and shoot rather than move anywhere. True, if you can establish a base of fire ("security element" in the kinder, gentler language of the times) to cover the threat from a distant and

To shoot while advancing, keep the head level by keeping the knees bent, and use a rolling gait when you step.

stationary point, this is fine. But realize that someone is eventually going to have to close with the suspect (I almost said enemy!) and take his ground. You may also find yourself in a tactically unsound position from which you must move while retaining your ability to fire. The skill of firing accurately while moving is essential to have in the "war bag" when the circumstances call for such a thing.

Moreover, if you are moving with other officers and have your entire team behind you, you cannot simply stop out in the

Other points for successful shooting on the move include an aggressive forward lean and keeping the elbows in tight, as in an SMG stance, for best weapon control.

If a threat is encountered to the support side while moving, it is a simple matter to turn at the waist and engage.

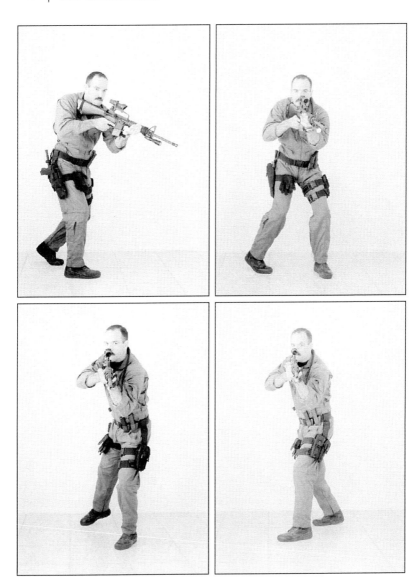

Engaging a threat on the primary side while on the move is slightly more difficult, depending on the angle. This may require a rapid repositioning of the entire body and firing platform in order to fire.

Quarter turns to engage an adversary on the support side begin by stepping forward with the outside leg and then pivoting toward the threat.

Threats to the primary side are handled the same way. Step toward the threat and pivot the body to orient the muzzle.

Half turns involve the same concepts. Step and then pivot toward the threat.

open. This will bottleneck everyone behind you as well as make it easier for the enem . . . err—"suspect" to shoot you. To be safe, you need the ability to shoot on the move.

As you move, you must adhere to the three eye principle. This means that except in specific situations, your eyes and your gun muzzle must always be oriented in the same direction. If you look up, your muzzle "looks" up also. If you look at the apex of a corner for a target indicator, your muzzle must be oriented toward that corner as well.

The objective is to be able to shoot any suddenly appearing threat without hesitation at all times—whether you are stationary, advancing, or passing the suspect on the move and shooting obliquely.

When you are moving through an open area, the walk to use is the tactical walk. In the tactical walk, you avoid exaggerating any of your movements or body mechanics. Walk just as you would walk down the street except for a few accommodations to the firearm you have in your hands. Your weapon will be up and oriented toward the point to which you are moving. Your knees will be slightly bent and you will have a slightly aggressive forward lean. This will help stabilize your upper body and allow a sort of rolling gait. It will also help avoid the common bouncing-up-and-down gait. The process looks like you are gliding, without any up and down motion, from one point to the next. Take smaller steps than you normally would in order to keep control of your feet and motion as you move. One U.S. Marine Corps (USMC) CQB instructor pointed out to me that the key is to move only as fast as you can guarantee getting hits on the hostile. Do not break into a run unless you are already under fire, since you cannot shoot effectively "on the run."

The firing position for this technique is very much like the firing position used with a submachine gun, rather than what would be traditionally used with a rifle. Your feet, knees, hips, and shoulders are squared to the target. Your primary-side foot will be trailing slightly to the rear. Your body will have a slightly aggressive forward lean, and your elbows will be pulled inward toward the ribcage. The rifle will be nearly in a firing position, although you will be holding the muzzle in a contact ready and looking over the sights.

Moving forward is not the only technique you must learn. It may be necessary to move directly from one point toward another, or even back up as you withdraw, while covering your flank with the muzzle of your weapon as you move.

Covering a potential danger area, or shooting to your support side as you move along a straight line is easy; all that is required is to pivot the body at the waist to the support side and point your weapon as you need it.

Covering a similar danger area or shooting to the strong/primary side on the move is slightly more difficult because of the inflexibility of the human torso and the upper body dynamics of most shooting positions. My training group has conducted some experiments in order to determine which method best solves this problem. The method I think is best, which I personally utilize, is to turn the body enough to allow a comfortable shooting position toward the danger area. This will actually turn you around 180 degrees from your line of travel, and now you simply move backward as you cover the danger area with your weapon.

The most important thing to remember is that the shooting platform exists from the waist upward. What the lower body and the feet are doing is almost inconsequential to your shooting. Isolate the shooting platform from the transportation (i.e., the legs).

These same concepts are as useful for evacuating an area as they are for "assaulting." If you are in a position where you want to get out of an area quickly, but you do not want to turn your back on danger areas, you can simply walk backward while keeping your weapon oriented toward the danger. Instead of walking heel-to-toe, you reverse it and walk toe-to-heel. This allows you to feel for unseen obstructions behind you as you move.

As you approach a particular danger area, such as the apex of a corner or a door, you may choose to slow down considerably and alter your gait accordingly. A technique that is useful in these cases is the "shuffle step." The advantage to this method is that it allows you to approach very carefully, slowly, and stealthily without compromising your position or ability to shoot. This method also discourages you from crossing your feet as you walk slowly. Crossing the feet during such a slow approach sometimes adversely affects your mobility and balance in tight quarters, as well as your ability to respond to various angles.

The shuffle step is as useful for moving forward and backward as it is for moving laterally. It is similar to the type of footwork that would be employed by a Western boxer. The leg that is closest to the desired direction moves first and is followed by a catch-up step with the other leg. Beginning with a slightly bladed Weaver stance, the footwork patterns are as follows. To move forward, take a half step forward with the support-side leg (front leg) and then catch up with a half step with the primary-side leg. To move rearward, reverse the process and begin with a half step rearward with the primary-side leg (rear leg) and then catch up with a half step with the support-side leg. To move laterally right or left the process is identical in concept.

Moving to the primary side (for a right-handed operator), take a half step to the right with the right leg and then catch up with the left leg. Reverse the process for the opposite direction.

Do not allow your feet to touch at midstep. Keep a slight distance (one-half shoulder width) between the feet on each step. A second common mistake is dragging the feet. Do not fall victim to this. Make the steps actual steps. Step with the toe first and then allow the heel to make contact with the deck. Remember that stealth is of the greatest importance when you are using this technique. Along with stability and enhanced potential for quick movement, this type of footwork allows you to clear an area using the angular search method without giving away your position.

CLOSE-CONTACT TECHNIQUES AND DRILLS

Shooting a rifle at 100 yards or more is a useful skill that the rifleman must have. Threats do materialize much closer, however, such as at arm's length. At such close quarters, hitting is still very important, but so is the speed of delivery. A close-proximity target can hit you with gunfire *very* quickly. Any knucklehead with a sawed-off, sightless, rusty SKS can send you on an early retirement to Valhalla if he's lucky enough . . . unless you shoot him first.

When extreme precision is required, you fire single, surgical shots. At close quarters, you don't need exact precision due to the size and proximity of the available target. What you want in such cases is incapacitation as instantly as possible. The preferred mode of fire within 10 yards is two shots, as quickly as you can keep them on target, into the thoracic (chest) cavity, followed by an immediate shot to the cranio-ocular cavity (head). The stance here is the prescribed SMG stance.

The reason you do not go for an immediate head shot (except under special circumstances) is that the chest is much easier to hit, thus beginning the damage process right away. The head shot becomes a follow-up shot. If you have prior knowledge of the suspect's use of armor or drugs, or if you have other information that leads you to expect a failure to stop, go for the head shot as a primary target. Remember, there are no guarantees!

Situations may arise where a close-quarters search or movement presents you with an adversary at arm's length. If the adversary chooses to fight, his chances of taking your rifle are great. This is something that neither you nor your brother officers can afford to have happen. You are quite justified in literally blowing him off the end of your rifle.

If you are at low ready or low inside ready and are faced with a threat, you will quickly realize that simply raising your rifle is not possible due to the proximity of the target. The solution is to execute a two-step technique that will create some standoff distance, allowing you to raise the rifle. Simultaneously, lift the rifle into a firing position or tuck it up under the arm in a close-contact firing position. Fire a quick-time pair to the body; step away again, perhaps to the side (shoulder the rifle if you initially fired from the close contact); and fire another quick-time pair, followed by a shot to the cranio-ocular cavity.

If you are being followed, dynamically, by your team and do not have the ability to move backward, there is an alternative. Simply jam the muzzle into the adversary's chest, as if you had a bayonet mounted on it. This may be enough to forestall his attack. If not, you are in a perfect position to continue as we discussed previously, except in *drive* instead of in *reverse*. This same series of drills may be executed to the right, left, and rear as needed.

There may be a need to respond to close-quarters threats to all angles along a 360-degree circle. Procedures have been in place for many years that enable operators to do this. The procedures, however, must not only be useful in a static environment, but also executable on the move. Examine the way you normally turn as you are walking from one point to another in a nontactical environment. This same procedure, with minor modifications to allow for the weapon system, is what you must use when moving with a rifle. Practice quarter and half turns with your rifle from various ready positions.

Another consideration in close quarters is the likelihood of multiple adversaries. Fear not! You have a rifle. The one consideration is to shoot each man once, thereby hurting them all as fast as you can, rather than shooting each one three times before going on to the next customer. Some authorities will say you should always shoot from left to right or right to left. This is totally unworkable in the real world. Sometimes you must shoot right to left; other times it will be reversed or inverted (inside targets first), depending on the adversary's positioning and attentional focus.

The rifle/carbine is a marvelously efficient and versatile weapon. It can reach *way* out there and enforce your will at a distance, yet it can also be your best asset when things get nasty up close.

Shooting at Angles

21

If I had worried about flanks, I could never have fought the war.
— Gen. George S. Patton Jr.

Shooting uphill or downhill is a very real possibility for police riflemen. There may be a circumstance where the best point to take is above the
line of sight of the suspect. If a shot is required, it
will be a downhill shot. Similarly, if you are called
to deploy against a sniper holdup on the third (or
higher) story of a building, any position you take
will likely be from below. It is important that you
understand how shooting at angles affects the
point of impact.

Instead of looking at the target on that high
incline (or decline) and trying to figure out the distance to the target, find out what the distance is to
the parallel surface the target is located in. For
example, if you have deployed across the street
from a building that is 50 yards away and there is

an armed criminal on the fifth floor, you can simply hold and shoot as if that criminal were 50 yards away. This is because gravity will only act on the bullet's horizontal flight at a 90-degree angle, regardless of the angle of departure.

The best solution to dealing with angled shots is to keep the distances close. Within 100 yards, it does not matter at what angle the suspect is positioned; the shot will not be affected more than 1.3 inches by the angle, and that is for the steepest angle of 60 degrees. Even at 200 yards, an unusually long shot from a police standpoint, the variance will not exceed 3 inches from point of impact on a flat range.

If the engagement distances are kept within 100 yards, you need not concern yourself with compensating for angles.

The Tactical Rifle in the CQB Environment

22

The laurels of victory are at the point of the enemy bayonets. They must be plucked there; they must be carried by hand-to-hand fight if one really means to conquer.
—Marshal of France Ferdinand Foch,
"Precepts and Judgements," 1919

Renewed police interest in the 5.56/.223 rifle has stimulated extensive testing for its possible use as an entry weapon in CQB environments. The fact that the round is not nearly as "overpenetrative" as police lore led many to believe, along with the long-range option and effectiveness against body armor, has caused many teams to rethink their choice of entry weapon.

The most commonly used SMG in SWAT circles is the H&K MP5 in its various configurations. Any weapon intended for entry/CQB duties must be compared to the MP5. The likely candidates to replace (or augment) the SMG are the short-barreled Colt Commando carbines, the Steyr AUG, and the H&K rifles in the same caliber.

The capacity of all the rifles in question is iden-

A short barrel has many advantages over longer barrels in close confines.

The HK MP5K/PDW, or any of its other versions, is often touted as the answer to close-quarters fighting. It excels at this role, but it cannot do what a .223 weapon can. Many teams are rethinking the role of their rifles and carbines. Mission needs must be examined before selecting weapons.

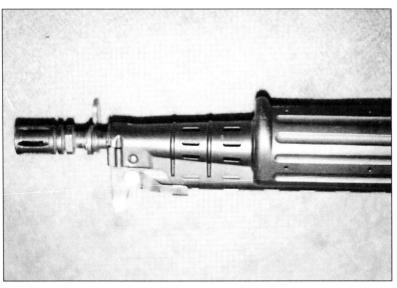

In spite of the attachment of flash suppressors, the muzzle blast and report will be much greater than that of the SMG.

tical to that of the SMG (maximum 30 rounds). The Colt has a slight advantage in that there are also 20-round magazines when space is limited.

The weight of the rifle should not be a factor, since most entry operators have superior upper body strength. This notwithstanding, the MP5 weighs about 7.5 pounds with a loaded magazine. The Colt weighs 8.5 pounds. The AUG weighs 9.5 pounds. In terms of length, the MP5 is about 27 inches, the AUG is 28 inches, and the other rifles (stocks extended) tape out at 35 inches. Clearly, the MP5 has the advantage of being short. This may not be as much of an advantage when you stop to consider that many operators will transition to the handgun for real close work. Even so, the longer weapons can work with slightly modified tactics.

The disadvantages of the 5.56/.223 in the indoors CQB environment include muzzle blast and flash. Certainly this is no more problematic than what is experienced from a short-barreled Benelli 12-gauge Entry Gun, but there are short sound suppressors and flash suppressors, such as the excellent Vortex series, that can be added without much fuss for those concerned.

Careful analysis of the ballistic effects of various rounds is mandatory. The entry role is not the same as a "general purpose" deployment. What works great in one may not have the desired effect in the other. Many teams, for example, have loaded their rifles with softpoint or hollowpoint ammunition for entry use, knowing the lessened penetration effects. Bullet weight must be examined carefully and kept light if the rifles will have shorter-than-usual barrels. For best efficiency, the 5.56/.223 requires a minimum velocity of approximately 2,500 fps.

The following additions to the entry carbine are required for maximum efficiency:

- *Light mount system.* For obvious reasons, any entry weapon must have an attached tactical white-light sys-tem. This is discussed at length in Chapter 19.
- *Tactical sling.* Again, discussed in the previous chapters, this is an essential addition. Without a sling, the opera-tor will not be able to transition, or to free up hands for other tasks.
- *Flash suppressor/sound suppressor.* You have not lived until you touch off a rifle (without flash suppressor) indoors! To say the effects are dramatic is an under-statement. Fortunately, most rifles worth considering for duty use come, as issued, with a flash suppressor. If they do not, one must be added. Vortex and Phantom flash suppressors are the best available, producing virtually no flash at all. These are available for virtually all mili-tary rifles and usually involve a simple screw-on instal-lation. Be sure to check the zero with the change in flash suppressor, just in case.

There are circumstances that may require the use of a sound suppressor. Suppressors are employed on rifles in the CQB environment to preserve the team's hearing and to enhance communications, not to hide the sound of gunshots. If

There are times in CQB operations when the presence of a sound suppressor is required. The overall length of the Steyr AUG is extended with a sound suppressor, but not by much. (Photo Courtesy of Cory Trapp, SAS Products.)

A Colt SMG with a sound suppressor. (Photo Courtesy of Cory Trapp, SAS Products.)

The ready positions used indoors are no different in concept than outdoors. At close quarters, be careful about the muzzle preceding your movements, but any other time, let your muzzle cover where your eyes are looking.

it's necessary to hide the source of (and minimize the report of) the rifle, then deploying with subsonic .223 ammo may be a viable option.

Teams have used suppressed rifles in confined environments such as department stores, airplane hangers, and other large buildings. Another use has been with teams that conduct entries into clandestine drug labs. The main advantages of the suppressed rifle (or SMG) are the suppression of any flash and/or gasses (important in drug lab entries) and the fact that the team will know if the shots fired have come from other team members or from the suspect(s). Realistic use will probably see the operator firing a small number of semiauto shots, but the unit must be able to withstand short, intermittent full-auto bursts. Ammunition selected will help in reducing flash. Federal ammunition seems to have the lowest flash signature.

The stance for shooting at CQB distances (within 7 yards) is more like the stance used in submachine gun training. Feet, knees, hips, and shoulders are squared on the target. The support foot is leading slightly, the knees are slightly bent, and the elbows are in, with an aggressive feel to the stance.

CQB is the natural home of full-auto fire. Jason Mann demonstrates the proper stance with a Micro Galil: weight slightly forward with an aggressive stance, elbows tucked inward, and trigger control yielding two- to three-round bursts.

With careful selection and some tactical modifications, the rifle can certainly be used inside. Doing so will give you greater tactical flexibility and, subsequently, greater survivability in the CQB environment.

Using the rifle indoors, or even in some outdoor close-quarters scenarios, may require fighting with the weapon in ultra-close quarters. In such circumstances, the rifle is used like a submachine gun. The firing position is more compressed and aggressive to allow you to move quickly and smoothly through small openings and doors and to engage threats quickly at close

In weapon retention situations, or when contact is likely at extreme contact distances, using the close contact position is a wise choice.

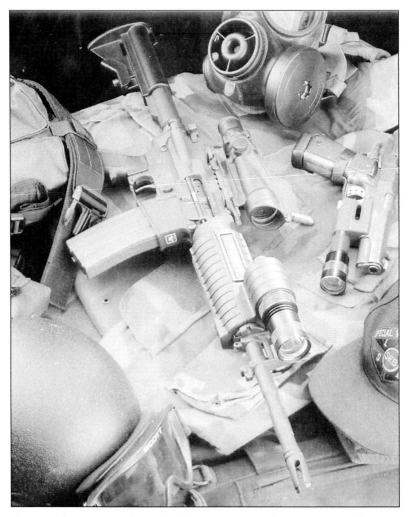

Extreme close quarters demands different equipment from the norm. Rifles (or SMGs) must have light mounts. Specialized optics are often an advantage in dark, close environments as well. (Photo Courtesy of Laser Products and SEB.)

range. In these scenarios, you may have to shoot at almost body-to-body contact, respond to threats on the move, and even execute weapon-retention techniques as you close on your adversaries. If chemical agents are deployed, you may also be required to fire with a gas mask in place. This is that area of the "big picture" where the rifle and submachine gun have nearly identical roles.

Suggested Qualification Course

23

1) Cold shot from a clean and dry bore (supported prone)
   50 yards
2) Five-shot group
   50 yards
3) Standards drills: shot from ready position/under time constraints

A)	7 yards	2 shots/failure to stop	1.5 seconds
B)	10 yards	2 shots	2.0 seconds
C)	10 yards	single shot/small targe	2.0 seconds
D)	15 yards	2 shots	2.5 seconds
E)	15 yards	single shot/small targe	2.5 seconds
F)	25 yards	2 shots	3.0 seconds
G)	25 yards	single shot/small target/ kneeling	4.0 seconds
H)	50 yards	single shot/squatting	4.0 seconds
I)	50 yards	single shot/kneeling	4.0 seconds
J)	75 yards	single shot/kneeling	5.0 seconds
K)	75 yards	single shot/sitting	6.0 seconds
L)	75 yards	single shot/prone	6.0 seconds
M)	100 yards	single shot/sitting	7.0 seconds
N)	100 yards	single shot/prone	7.0 seconds

Continuous and proper training in fundamental basic riflecraft is essential to all personnel who are so equipped.

All on-duty training should be administered by knowledgeable officers schooled in tactical (as opposed to "sport" or "hunting") rifle techniques.

Both precision and CQB drills must be a part of the overall education of a police rifle operator.

A tactical rifle officer must be capable of engagements out to 100 yards.

4) Gun handling drills: no shooting, done against time
   Overtime execution deducts 2 points from score.

A)	Tactical reload	3X	6.0 seconds
B)	Speed load	3X	4.0 seconds
C)	Failure to fire	3X	2.0 seconds
D)	Failure to eject	3X	2.0 seconds
E)	Feedway stoppage	3X	6.0 seconds
F)	Transition to pistol	3X	3.0 seconds

25 shots total (each is worth 4 points). Possible score is 100 points.

Course is shot on any realistically sized humanoid silhouette target. A center hit is worth four points, and a peripheral hit is worth two points. The cold shot and the five-shot group are not timed and must be within specified standards.

CARBINE TEN

Begin with a single target or steel silhouette 200 yards away from the shooter. On command, the shooter drops to prone and engages the target twice. He gets up and runs to 150 yards, where he again engages twice from prone. He gets up and runs to 100 yards and engages twice from sitting. Again, he gets up and runs to 50, where he engages from any position other than sitting or prone. Finally, he runs to 25 yards, where he engages for two head shots from standing.

The entire run is timed from start until the last shots are fired. Any misses will add 10 seconds to the time, and any peripheral hits add 5 seconds. The man with the best overall time is top gun. Establishing a par-time for the team can even serve as a qualification/obstacle course of sorts.

Record Keeping and the Data Book

24

The data or record book is intended to help you keep track of your development as a shooter, to point out areas that require greater focus, and finally to insure that your equipment is working as expected. It may even become a legal document later to demonstrate the degree of precision and the level of commitment that you are capable of.

You are expected to fill out one sheet of the book at every training session. You will log the information and later have an ongoing record of how your weapon/ammo combination works in varying weather conditions, as well as varying light conditions. It will also be a record of what you've learned in your training sessions.

A rifleman's log book not only is a record of his development as a rifleman, but also is a record of his experience and ability. It may become an important document in court if a rifle deployment results in litigation.

TACTICAL RIFLE TEAM LOG BOOK

DATE _____ RANGE LOCATION _____

TEMPERATURE_____ LIGHTING _____

TIME _____ WIND VALUES _____

WEAPON _____ AMMO AND LOT_____

COLD SHOT

POSITION_____

DISTANCE _____

DISTANCE FROM POA _____

ADJUSTMENTS _____

AFFIX COLD SHOT
TARGET TO
REVERSE SIDE

5-SHOT GROUP

POSITION _____

DISTANCE _____

DISTANCE FROM POA _____

GROUP SIZE _____

AFFIX 5-SHOT
GROUP TARGET
TO REVERSE
SIDE

STANDARD DRILLS AND NOTES:

Final Thoughts: Selecting the Rifleman

25

Of every One-Hundred men, Ten shouldn't even be there,
Eighty are nothing but targets,
Nine are real fighters . . .
We are lucky to have them . . . They make the battle.
Ah but the One, One of them is a Warrior . . . and He will bring the others back.
—Hericletus c. 500 B.C.

In selecting personnel for a rifle team, whether as part of a patrol team or as individual rifle-equipped officers, it is imperative to put the square peg in the square hole. This means that if you want to succeed at the mission, you must select those with the right aptitude, not to mention the right attitude, to become riflemen. The rifle magnifies an officer's life-and-death responsibilities. Incorrect, careless, or politically motivated assignment of personnel to a rifle team may cost you and the agency more than you can possibly imagine.

Some agencies have little faith in their line personnel and give the rifles only to "trusted" supervisors. They seem to think that chevrons on the sleeves automatically convey tactical knowledge and marksmanship skill. This, of course, is as ridiculous as the idea that single-officer cars are somehow "safer" than two-officer cars!

Other agencies take the other extreme and follow the "warm body" egalitarian approach, issuing rifles to anyone and everyone—with no regard for ability and with virtually no training! This is just as negligent. Many officers may not be interested or dedicated enough to develop and maintain the skills needed to operate the rifle. To give a rifle to a man (or woman) who is not skilled or who will not train with it or, worse yet, who has not come to terms with the reality of using it on a suspect, is a problem waiting to happen.

A far better path than either extreme is to allow the prospective rifleman to self-select. By that I mean to set stringent requirements and allow those interested to volunteer. A selection process may include such things as a physical agility test, a marksmanship test, and even an oral interview. The physical ability issue is important because the rifle is a physical weapon, and it is ill suited for the feeble or physically weak. Prior shooting experience is desirable but not essential. It is easier to teach an experienced shooter to become an excellent shooter than it is to teach a neophyte to be adequate. Finally, an oral interview regarding shooting incidents, policy, and even case law regarding deadly force and other agency-specific issues is important. Equally important in such an interview is determining how the prospective rifle officer feels about using justified deadly force. Many readers would be surprised at just how many officers *will not shoot under ANY circumstances!* Such an officer has no business with a rifle.

A self-selecting rifleman (yes, women also make great *riflemen*, but "rifle-person" is a cumbersome word) will be the sort of officer who is already physically fit. He is the sort of officer who never has any trouble "qualifying" with other weapons and is perhaps a tactics student or member of the SWAT unit.

Another attribute that is essential, but less apparent in officers every year, is coolness under fire. *Past performance is the best indicator of future performance*, and coolness is only developed with experience. A rifleman should be a seasoned and experi-

The rifle magnifies an officer's life and death responsibility.

enced officer, not a wet-behind-the-ears academy grad whose
dad is on good terms with someone in city hall. An experienced
and seasoned officer who is cool as a popsicle under fire is worth
five other officers. If such a man is also a good shot, he is worth
ten other officers. This view may not be popular with our current
collective "anyone-can-be-trained-to-do-anything-because-we-
are-all-essentially-the-same" mentality, but it is the plain truth.

Unfortunately, such men and women are often labeled the
Dobermans and rottweilers of law enforcement and are delib-
erately deselected by those who've never risked anything more
than a paper cut from the Xerox machine or a head cold from
their office air conditioner. Such practice is a disservice to
everyone from the officer himself to the citizenry and the
department as a whole. To quote a senior command staff officer
at a large urban southern California police agency, "There is no
clean, nice, or politically correct way to arrest an armed, violent,
and homicidal criminal who does not want to be arrested." He
is quite correct. You need the Dobermans and rottweilers of the
police community for such duty! Be glad you have them! If you
don't agree, consider the following.

Imagine your son or daughter (or anyone else who is more important to you than life itself) held by a wild-eyed, drugged-up, madman armed with an ax. Surrounded by untrained and hesitant police officers and tired of negotiating, he is about to cut your child's leg off with the razor-edged ax! Across the street, hidden in the shadows, is a lone police rifleman. He's been there for an hour, waiting for the right moment . . . waiting for the criminal to expose himself. Now he has the madman in his scope, and his trigger finger is the only thing standing between your child's safety and the gruesome and bloody death the suspect has planned for him or her. (The above incident actually occurred!) Now ask yourself this, and be honest. *Who do you want taking the shot?* 1) Do you want an untested rookie who has never shot an actual suspect, who is so stressed out that he is about to piss his pants, and who is not really sure if he *can, if he should . . . or even if he WILL shoot?!* 2) Or do you want a seasoned veteran who's been in combat a number of times, who will calmly and easily make the shot, and who is thinking, "I've done this before, and, by God, I am going to do it again."?

We all know the answer don't we? For you police administrators out there, you have an even more thankless job than the operators, but you certainly bear no less responsibility. Select your people as if your family's lives depended on it . . . someday they might! If your intent is to place a rifle in every car, then make certain that your personnel are trained well in how to deploy it. Such things cannot be left to chance.

And, for you experienced operators out there, those of you who're on a first-name basis with *Ol' Jumbo the elephant*, heed this little bit of advice. Record every bit of information you can about every single tactical deployment, and keep it at home in a safe. Virtually all armed encounters will be resolved without incident or shooting. The incidents where you were required to shoot, however, are the only ones that "some of *those* people" will remember and focus on.

You, as an operator, should not have any problem with shooting when it is justified and required (if you do, you are in the wrong line of work), but others, undoubtedly, will. As one who has been in your shoes, let me tell you that the day will come when some . . . "person" will accuse you of being everything from a baby killer to a head-hunting, Godless, cannibal heathen because you've done your job professionally and dispassionately. The bottom line is that you remind "those people" of what they are not and can never be and of the courage that they lack. Your mere existence is forever a condemnation to them, and if they can make your life and career difficult for you, they will. Having a computer file with 50 times as many non-shooting deployments as you have had shooting incidents will help keep the administrative liability and civil liability in check. This is also a good idea for entire departments, as no one wants to be accused of being trigger-happy.

I cannot take credit for that idea, as I learned it from an old K-9 officer with many, many "deployments" under his belt. He keeps track of every single time his K-9 partner is deployed. The nonbites far outnumber the bites. Showing this to a jury or overzealous internal affairs investigator or even justifiably inquisitive command personnel will tend, he says, to keep things in their proper perspective.

If you are an operator-turned-administrator in the process of establishing a rifle program, do your agency a favor and don't turn it into a ticket-punching assignment or a money/bonus position, and certainly don't fill it with inexperienced personnel. Cultivate your experienced volunteers/officers, allow them to polish their rifle skills, and let them select themselves as the core of your rifle program. Train everyone who will be deploying with the rifle to the best of their ability, and then trust them to do what you hired them to do. You will be allowing the best officers to do the job. You will be glad you did when the first shot is fired . . . trust me.

Appendix
Suggested Reading and References

BOOKS

Crews, Jim. *Some of the Answer.* Arizona: Crews Publications, 1997.

Cooper, Jeff. *Art of the Rifle.* Boulder: Paladin Press, 1997.

Fairburn, Richard. *Police Rifles.* Boulder: Paladin Press, 1994.

HK International Training Division. *Sniper Instructor Course,* class notebook, Sterling, VA: Heckler & Koch, 1998.

LAPD. *SWAT Firearms Shooting Manual,* Section V: "The Urban Rifle." Unpublished, 1993.

LAPD. *Tactical Shotgun Shooting Manual.* Unpublished, 1996.

LASD. *SEB Long Rifle School Notebook.* Unpublished, 1993.

LASD. *SWAT School Notebook.* Unpublished, 1993.

Long, Duncan. *HK Assault Rifle Systems.* Boulder: Paladin Press, 1996.

La Garde, Col. Louis A. *Gunshot Injuries.* Mt. Ida, Arkansas: Lancer Militaria, 1991.

Suarez, Gabriel. *Tactical Pistol.* Boulder: Paladin Press, 1995.

Suarez, Gabriel. *Tactical Shotgun.* Boulder: Paladin Press, 1996.

Suarez, Gabriel. *Tactical Advantage.* Boulder: Paladin Press, 1997.

Suarez, Gabriel. *SMPD Tactical Rifle Team Manual.* Unpublished, 1998

USMC, Dept. of the Navy. M16A2 Service Rifle Sustainment Training Program. Washington, D.C.: 1996.

MAGAZINES

International Wound Ballistics Review. All Issues and specifically articles by Martin Fackler. IWBA, P.O. Box 701, El Segundo, CA 90245.

ARTICLES

Fackler, Dr. Martin. "Gunshot Wounds Review." Annals of Emergency Medicine 28:2 (August 1996): 194–203.

McPherson, Duncan. ".223 Ammunition for Law Enforcement." *IWBA Wound Ballistics Review* 3:2, 30–33.

Roberts, Dr. Gary K. and Special Agent Michael R. Bullian. "Comparison of the Wound Ballistic Potential of 9mm vs. 5.56mm (.223) Cartridges for Law Enforcement Entry Applications." *AFTE Journal* 25:2 (April 1993): 142–146.

Robertson, Lt. Stephen C. "Rifle Ammunition Performance through Barriers." IWBA Wound Ballistics Review 2:4, 25–34.

Williams, Gary W. "12 Gauge Shotshell & .223 Caliber Rifle Ammunition Performance through House Trailer Barriers." *IWBA Wound Ballistics Review* 3:3, 29–32.

RECOMMENDED TRAINING COURSES

HALO Group, Inc., Tactical Training
(www.thehalogroup.com)

- Tactical Rifle Course
- Tactical Submachine Gun/.223 Rifle Course
- Tactical Rifle Instructor School
- MP5 Intermediate Operator's Course
- MP5/SMG Advanced Operators Course
- MP5 Instructor's Course
- CQB Rifle for the Advanced Operator Course
- Advanced Law Enforcement Military SniperCourse

FBI Counter Sniper Course

Heckler & Koch International Training Division
(www.hecklerkoch-usa.com)

- Rifle Instructor Course
- Tactical Rifle Course
- Tactical Submachine Gun Course

LASD AR-15 Rifle School
LASD SEB Long Rifle/Sniper School
SMPD Patrol Tactical Rifle School

About the Author

Gabriel Suarez is a veteran of Southern California law enforcement, where he has served for many years. His extensive field experience includes single officer patrol, gang enforcement, and special operations. He also serves as tactical trainer for his agency. He was one of the founding members of his department's Special Weapons and Tactical Precision Rifle teams. In 1991 he was awarded the Police Medal of Valor for his actions during a critical incident. He is still active in the law enforcement profession, as well as in the training industry. This is his fourth book on tactical training and deployment issues.